PRINCE
in comics

Writer
Tony Lourenço

Art
Joël Alessandra
Céheu
Christopher
Samir Dahmani
Anne Defréville
Samuel Figuière
Baudouin Forget
Noémie Honein
Kongkee
Yvan Ojo
Christelle Pécout
Barrack Rima
Toru Terada
Léah Touitou
Martin Trystram
Yunbo

Cover
Christopher

Text chapters
Nicolas Finet

Graphic Design
Romain Nélis

Translation
Montana Kane

nbm GRAPHIC NOVELS
Nantier · Beall · Minoustchine
NEW YORK

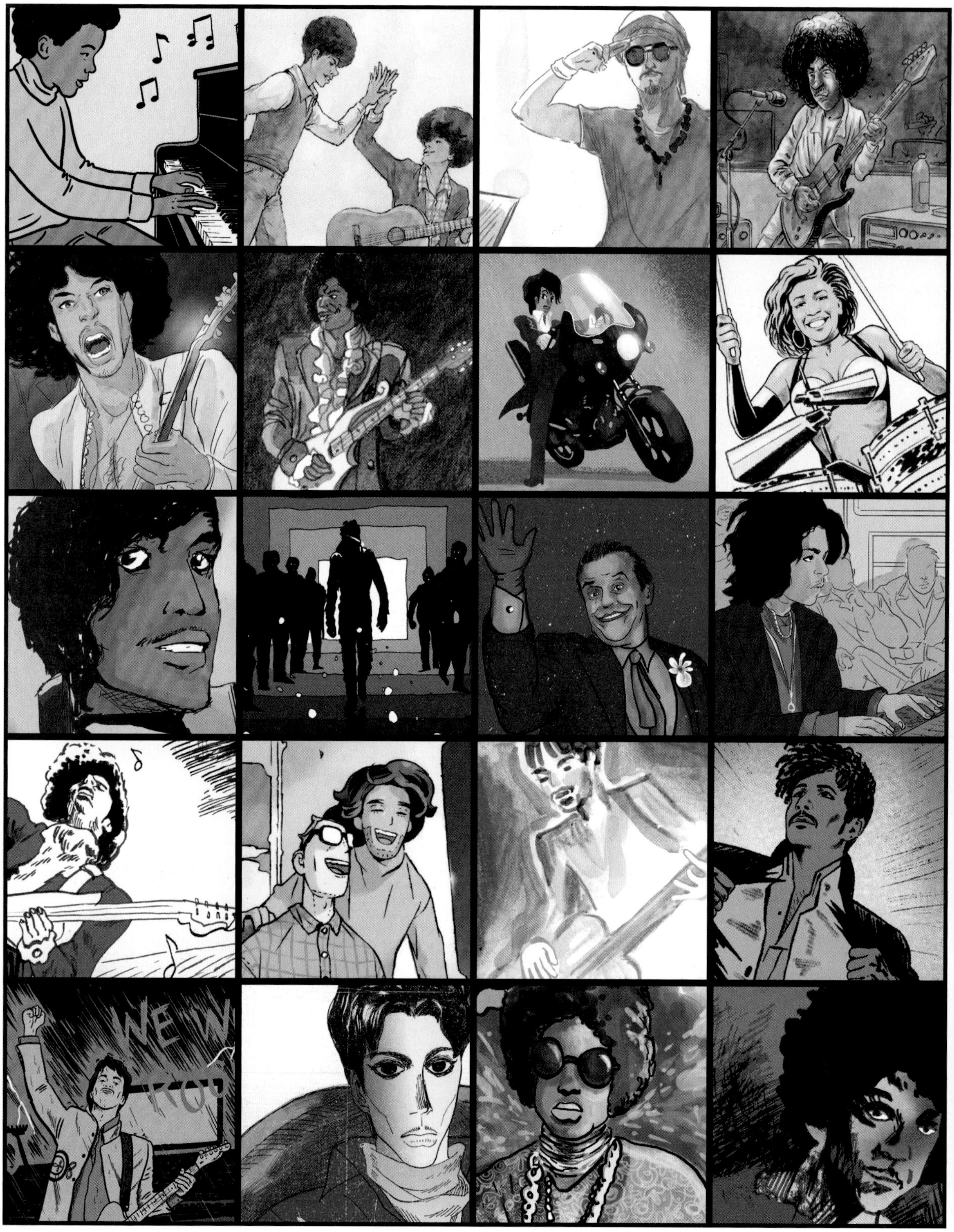

ISBN 9781681123219
© 2021 Editions Petit à Petit
© 2023 NBM for the English translation

Library of Congress Control Number 2023936218
Further credits on back page

THE 1960s

WAY UP NORTH...

Contrary to the glamorous clichés associated with the mythical cities of American pop music, it's cold in Minneapolis, Minnesota, and, at the time, there were few black people. Yet it was there, in a household, which, though it dissolved early on, was inhabited by the spirit of music, that Prince Rogers Nelson grew up, the strange child destined for an extraordinary future.

ART : Christopher

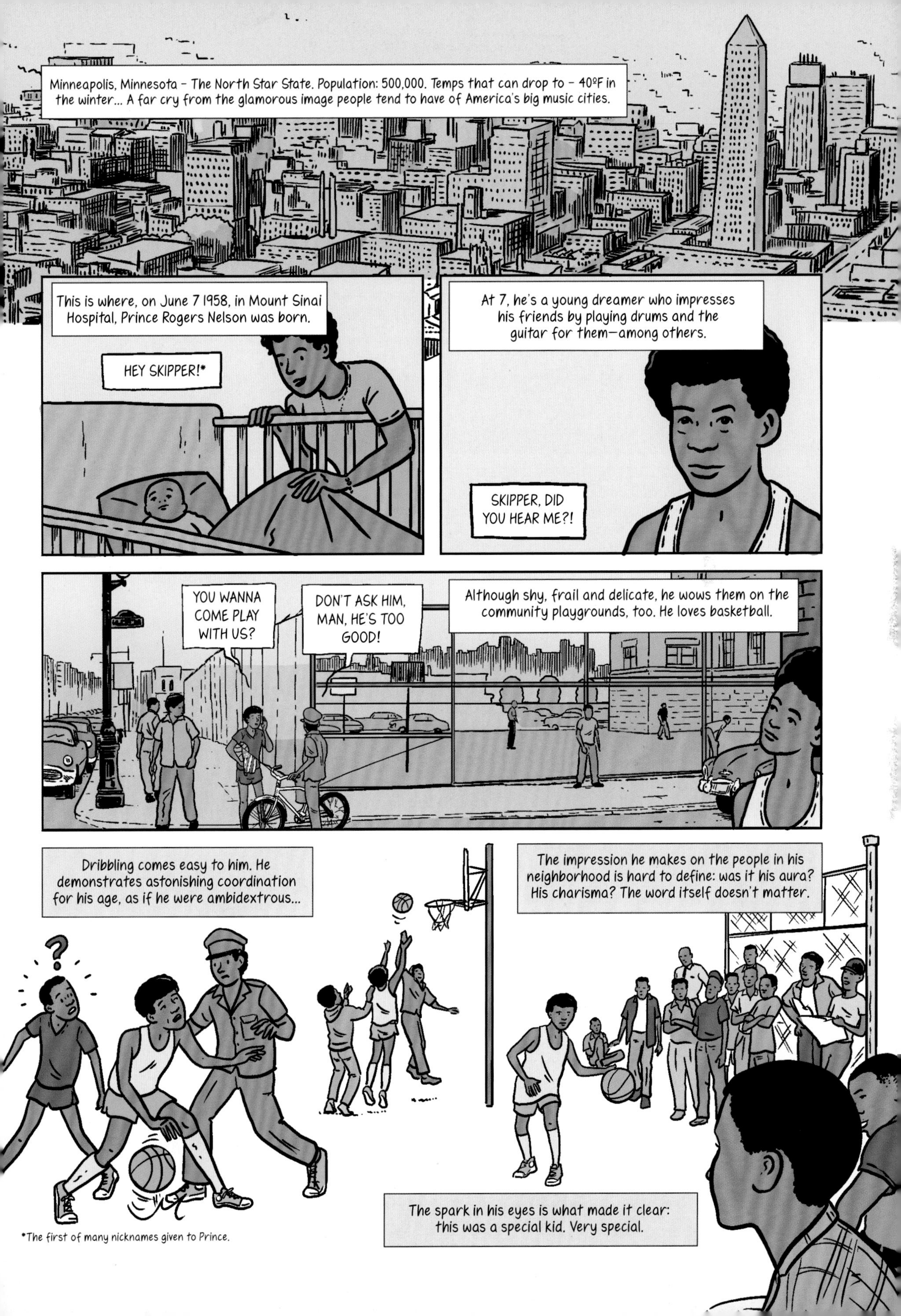
Minneapolis, Minnesota – The North Star State. Population: 500,000. Temps that can drop to – 40ºF in the winter... A far cry from the glamorous image people tend to have of America's big music cities.
This is where, on June 7 1958, in Mount Sinai Hospital, Prince Rogers Nelson was born.
HEY SKIPPER!*
At 7, he's a young dreamer who impresses his friends by playing drums and the guitar for them—among others.
SKIPPER, DID YOU HEAR ME?!
YOU WANNA COME PLAY WITH US?
DON'T ASK HIM, MAN, HE'S TOO GOOD!
Although shy, frail and delicate, he wows them on the community playgrounds, too. He loves basketball.
Dribbling comes easy to him. He demonstrates astonishing coordination for his age, as if he were ambidextrous...
?
The impression he makes on the people in his neighborhood is hard to define: was it his aura? His charisma? The word itself doesn't matter.
The spark in his eyes is what made it clear: this was a special kid. Very special.
*The first of many nicknames given to Prince.

He got his first name, Prince, from his father, John L. Nelson.

John was a plasterer who moved north to Minneapolis to escape the racism in the south.

Prince's mother, Mattie, had just finished college when she met John, who was sixteen years her senior.

After graduation, she began work as community activist and married John.

They had two children together: Prince Rogers and, two years later, Tyka Evene.

John was also a brilliant jazz musician who regularly performed in the clubs around town, often accompanied by Mattie on vocals.

AND TONIGHT, AT THE PIANO...

His passion for music led him to name his son after the character he played in his jazz band, aptly named...

...PRINCE ROGERS!

Prince would stay up for hours...

...listening to his parents.

Those were magical moments.

But in the Nelson household, not all moments were magical.

JOHN, I NEED TO TAKE A BREAK. I--

BUT WE *JUST* STARTED!

I NEED TO CLEAN THE HOUSE AND DO LAUNDRY.

YOU'LL HAVE PLENTY OF TIME TO DO THAT LATER!

IT'S ALWAYS THE SAME. WE START REHEARSING AND THEN TEN MINUTES LATER, HER HIGHNESS SPLITS!

WELL THEN HELP ME WITH THE HOUSEWORK!

SURE! BUT THEN WHO'S GONNA BRING HOME HE DOUGH, HUH?!

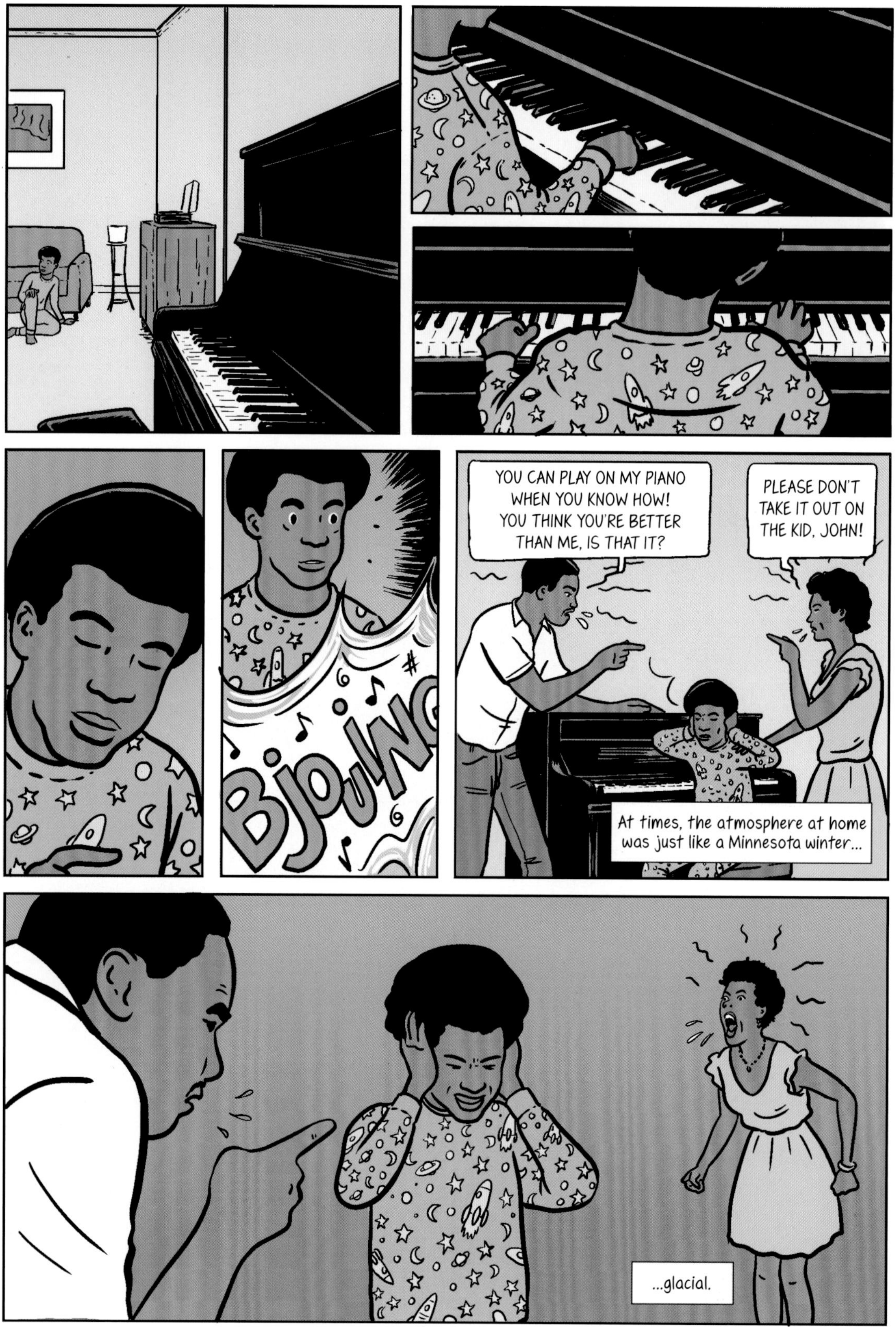
Bjouing
YOU CAN PLAY ON MY PIANO WHEN YOU KNOW HOW! YOU THINK YOU'RE BETTER THAN ME, IS THAT IT?
PLEASE DON'T TAKE IT OUT ON THE KID, JOHN!
At times, the atmosphere at home was just like a Minnesota winter...
...glacial.

The divorce was finalized on September 24, 1968.

John left the family home, taking all his things with him: his clothes, knick-knacks...all his belongings.

Except one.

Young Prince was now determined to play as well as his father.

Self-taught...

...with music his sole obsession.

His mother watched the prodigy bloom, witnessing, on a daily basis her son's creative power...

...waiting to reach the timelessness of genius.

W hat on Earth were they doing there, way up North? In the 1950s, Minneapolis, MN was the last place one would have expected to witness the birth of an innovative new music scene. When it comes to music, most people think of New York, Los Angeles – even Chicago or Detroit, especially in terms of the blues, jazz, R&B, soul and more. But... Minneapolis, *really?!* North, where at the time, African-Americans represented barely 2% of the population,

BORN INTO A DYSFUNCTIONAL FAMILY, YOUNG PRINCE ROGERS NELSON SOUGHT REFUGE IN MUSIC, INSPIRED BY A FATHER WHOM HE ADMIRED IN SPITE OF IT ALL. MUSICAL ENERGY WOULD BE HIS SALVATION AND PASSPORT TO ADULTHOOD.

who clearly took good care of herself; John was a handsome man, and the very image of maturity. During the day, he worked at Honeywell Electronics, where he molded plastic. But in the evening, in the clubs, he dazzled audiences as the piano player in a jazz band, the Prince Rogers Trio.

John was sixteen years older than Mattie. Suffice to say that he had plenty of time to have another life before her. He was pleasing to the ladies and not one to let fidelity get in the way. When he married Mattie, he already had three children from a previous relationship – and it wouldn't stop there: eventually, Prince would have a grand total of six half-siblings, in addition to John and Mattie's other child, his sister Tika Evene.

Minneapolis today, adjacent to the capital of Minnesota, Saint Paul.

that John Lewis Nelson and Mattie Della Shaw, the parents of the hero of this history, made their home-- perhaps precisely to keep at bay the most unpleasant effects of the intense segregation of which African Americans were then victims.

Few details regarding the exact circumstances in which they met have survived, but there remain photos from that period. Mattie was a pretty, outgoing woman

Prince's house in the late 60s.

When Prince Rogers Nelson was born on June 7, 1958 at Mount Sinai Hospital, Mattie was twenty-five. The Nelsons lived at 915 Logan Avenue in a neighborhood in North Minneapolis, a modest and densely populated environment but not a disadvantaged one. "The house of my childhood: it was all pink (...) The furniture was rudimentary. I remember this funky energy that emanated from it. The people, the voices, the energy. Just like the Kennedys, but Black." wrote Prince in *The Beautiful Ones*, his unfinished memoir.

For music was there, early on; it was everywhere. John on keyboard, Mattie on vocals. Magic? Probably, but not for very long. Disagreements began to turn into fights. And John had a tendency to hit, unfortunately. The young Skipper (one of Prince's many nicknames over the years) was only seven years old when his parents divorced. Less than three years later, Mattie remarried a man from Chicago, Hayward Baker. This stepfather would make life miserable for the young boy - to the point that he left his new home to go back to live with his father the piano player. Does the fact that he spent his childhood being shuffled between homes account for the artist's fragility? It is common knowledge that as a child he had epilepsy - and that the symptoms disappeared abruptly, without explanation. We also know that Prince's singularity was expressed very early on. People who knew him have mentioned a hyperactive, disturbing, somewhat strange child. In short, he was different.

That, reinforced no doubt by his diminutive physique, would be a source of mockery directed at him. But against all odds, he managed to draw from that mockery the strength to resist, alone against the world, and to retaliate by using a haughty attitude against his oppressors--an attitude, which, even after he found fame and fortune, would never completely leave him. And then there was his incredible creative energy. He is said to have composed his first title, *Funk Machine*, at the tender age of seven. But this can't be verified, of course, much like a good part of what he himself would peddle throughout his existence about his own life story, striving to cover his tracks and confuse people.

Aren't the best stories the ones we make up?

THE 70s
ANDRÉ AND ME

Deeply shaken by a difficult relationship with his parents, young Prince, still a pre-teen, seeks refuge in music of all kinds, eagerly absorbing everything he encounters. This will be one of the keys to his future creative eclecticism—that and the deep bond he forms with his first long-term musical sidekick, André Cymone.

ART : Yunbo

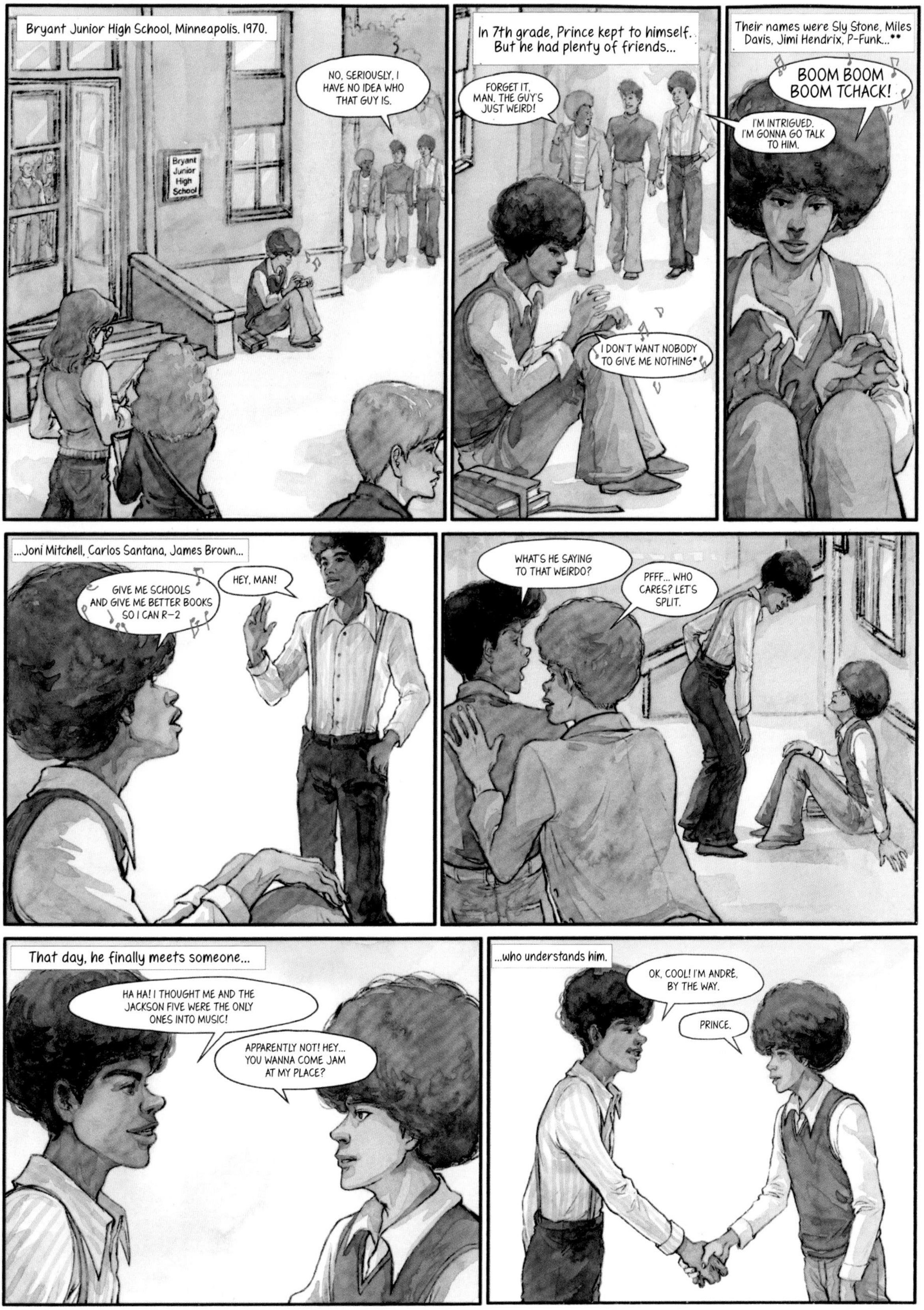
Bryant Junior High School, Minneapolis. 1970.
Bryant Junior High School
NO, SERIOUSLY, I HAVE NO IDEA WHO THAT GUY IS.
In 7th grade, Prince kept to himself. But he had plenty of friends...
FORGET IT, MAN. THE GUY'S JUST WEIRD!
I DON'T WANT NOBODY TO GIVE ME NOTHING*
Their names were Sly Stone, Miles Davis, Jimi Hendrix, P-Funk...**
BOOM BOOM BOOM TCHACK!
I'M INTRIGUED. I'M GONNA GO TALK TO HIM.
...Joni Mitchell, Carlos Santana, James Brown...
GIVE ME SCHOOLS AND GIVE ME BETTER BOOKS SO I CAN R-2
HEY, MAN!
WHAT'S HE SAYING TO THAT WEIRDO?
PFFF... WHO CARES? LET'S SPLIT.
That day, he finally meets someone...
HA HA! I THOUGHT ME AND THE JACKSON FIVE WERE THE ONLY ONES INTO MUSIC!
APPARENTLY NOT! HEY... YOU WANNA COME JAM AT MY PLACE?
...who understands him.
OK, COOL! I'M ANDRÉ, BY THE WAY.
PRINCE.

*"I DON'T WANT NOBODY TO GIVE ME NOTHING" BY JAMES BROWN.
**PARLIAMENT-FUNKADELIC.

At Prince's home – 915 Logan Avenue, in a quiet, middleclass black neighborhood.

WOW, MAN, YOU'RE REALLY GOOD!

LEMME SEE THAT BASS.

OKAY, BUT THIS IS JUST AN OLD FOUR-STRING I TINKERED WITH, SO...

For André Anderson, this jam session is a revelation.

The two aspiring musicians really hit it off.

I FOUND THIS BLACK RADIO STATION, AND THIS OTHER ONE THAT PLAYS ALTERNATIVE ROCK, WHICH I LOVE! BUT I COULDN'T FIND ANY SOUL STATIONS.

YEAH, ME NEITHER, SO I JUST LISTEN TO ALBUMS AND I INVENT MY OWN SOUNDS.

It becomes clear...

THE BASS IS WHAT I LOVE MOST... I GOT THAT FROM MY OLD MAN!

HA HA! MY OLD MAN'S A MUSICIAN TOO, HE'S IN A JAZZ BAND.

...that the two share...

CHECK IT OUT, THAT'S HIM A FEW YEARS AG--

HOLY CRAP!

THAT'S MY OLD MAN THERE, RIGHT NEXT TO YOURS! THEY PLAYED IN THE SAME BAND!

...a strong connection.

1244 Russell Avenue. Prince spends a lot of time at André's house, a 10-minute walk away...

BETWEEN MY OLD MAN, MY STEP-DAD, AND MY MOM... IT'S NOT EASY, I'M CONSTANTLY BEING SHUFFLED AROUND.

...from the home he no longer lived in.

RIGHT NOW I'M CRASHING AT MY AUNT OLIVIA'S, BUT I THINK SHE'S GETTING SICK OF ME.

HEH HEH... LOOKS LIKE I'M GETTING A NEW ROOMMATE!

André is the youngest of six children. But his mom, Bernadette, welcomes Prince with open arms.

The two friends set up camp in the basement.

"FUNKMACHINE"?

YEP, THE FIRST PIECE I WROTE! I WAS SEVEN AT THE TIME!

DAMN YOU'RE GOOD, BRO!

...where they can really get into it...

ANDRÉ, YOU KNOW WHAT WE SHOULD DO?

...like two brothers.

START OUR OWN BAND!

That goal is achieved in 1971. Prince on keyboard and guitar, André on bass, and both of them doing vocals. A cousin of Prince, Charles "Chazz" Smith, becomes the band's drummer.

The trio quickly expands, with Terry Jackson and William Doughy on percussions and then André's sister Linda on keyboard.

Chazz being the oldest, he is the de facto leader.

SO WE'RE NOT CHARLES'S COUSINS & FRIENDS ANYMORE?

NOPE. WE'RE THE PEOPLE'S CHURCH!

And as such, he frequently changes the name of the band without telling the others.

At a local contest once, our young artists thought they were performing as Soul Explosion and lost to another band called...

IIIIT'S.... PHOENIIIIIX!

LET'S GIVE THEM A BIG HAND!

THAT SUCKS!

Except that they weren't Soul Explosion that night, but... Phoenix.

YES! HA HA!

Chazz had renamed them the day before.

This little game went on until the true boss spoke up in 1973.

IN MEMORY OF OUR HIGH SCHOOL, CENTRAL HIGH, AND AS A TRIBUTE TO GRAND FUNK RAILROAD, OUR NEW NAME IS NOW...

...GRAND CENTRAL.

In those days, there was practically one band per block in Minneapolis, and despite mutual respect, competition was fierce. Most notably, there was The Family*, with Sonny Thomson and the Lewis brothers. Big talents. Big style.

But with Prince as a member, Grand Central becomes huge.

The musicians dazzle on stage. They all play multiple instruments and even trade them during a concert for effect.

They usually rehearse at Terry's house. It's big and he lives there alone with his parents. Meanwhile, Prince is taking over the band.

WE GOTTA GET THIS RIGHT, RIGHT *NOW!* IF THE LOCALS DON'T LIKE IT, WE AIN'T GOING ANYWHERE, GUYS!

I DON'T WANT TO SOUND LIKE ANYONE ELSE. I DON'T WANNA JUST DO SONGS AS IS, LIKE A JUKEBOX.

YEAH, WE GOTTA ADD EFFECTS AND RIFFS AND THINK OUTSIDE THE BOX, MAN!

WE CAN BE AS GOOD AS THE JACKSON FIVE!

After a while, they kick Chazz out of the band. He kept "forgetting" to divvy up the money after Grand Central gigs.

IT'S 'CAUSE THERE WERE EXPENSES, GUYS!

He's replaced by Morris Day, who's cooler plus has his own gear. His mother ends up managing the band.

Grand Central starts playing more and more original songs and gradually builds a reputation.

André Anderson becomes André Cymone, a stage name inspired by his middle name, Simon.

As for Prince, he glows. The skinny shy kid has donned his new costume...

...as the Kid from Minneapolis.

* FORMERLY BACK TO BLACK.

The austere facade of the middle school where Prince and André became friends.

In middle school, no one bothered to approach the weird little guy standing over there by himself. He didn't say much and wasn't very popular, to say the least. It was obvious that he was smart and aware of what was going on around him- but then again, who could really tell what was going through the mind of that featherweight freak, huh? One of the students from Bryant Junior High School, however, would brave the unknown to approach this intriguing loner. Andre Simon Anderson, who was twenty days younger than Prince, already knew who he was, actually, but from afar. His parents, Fred and Bernadette, attended the same church (the Seventh-day Adventist Church) as the Nelsons, and no doubt the two families sometimes crossed paths there. But this time it was a little more than a fleeting contact. Like many teenagers from countries everywhere and from any time period, the discovery of music is what helped them bond very quickly. And it wasn't just Black music, which, at the dawn of the 1970s, didn't come close to having the kind of audience it does today. The two new friends were just as much into Smokey Robinson, James Brown, Duke Ellington and Earth, Wind and Fire as they were into Steely Dan, Chicago, Joni Mitchell, Grand Funk Railroad, the Doobie Brothers and West Coast jazz. They remembered and absorbed everything, like sponges taking

> THROUGHOUT AN ADOLESCENCE AFFECTED BY THE TURBULENCE OF A DYSFUNCTIONAL FAMILY, THE YOUNG PRINCE CLUNG TO HIS CLOSE FRIEND ANDRE ANDERSON FOR SUPPORT. THE BOYS WERE BOTH CRAZY ABOUT MUSIC AND WENT ON TO INVENT A DESTINY TOGETHER.

Duke Ellington

in all the trends, as one tends to do at that age. They found common ground in the programs they listened to on the radio: funk on the local black radio station KUXL or white rock on KQRS. Soon, it became about more than just listening to music and developed into making it, as well. Because in the meantime, yet another change of residence had occurred in the life of young Prince. The constant bickering with his father John led the young boy to

he turned into his personal and musical kingdom. This arrangement would last for years. That basement was where the two boys, Prince and Andre, practiced their music and, bursting with self-confidence, formed their first band, which they called Grand Central Corporation, in honor of bass player Larry Graham, a former member of Sly and the Family Stone who went on to form his own band, Graham Central Station.

The young band Grand Central, in the days when they dreamed of conquering the U.S. charts. Prince is the next to last one on the right.

seek refuge with his aunt Olivia. But that didn't last either, and eventually, it was in the home of his new friend Andre, 1244 Russell Avenue, that he settled in for good. Andre's mother, Bernadette Anderson, was a divorcée already raising her six children alone. She was a pillar of the Black community, resilient, well-known and respected. Bernadette was impressive, strong and independent. And she had a generous spirit: she agreed to take in this additional pre-teen in need of a real home. He moved into the basement, which

The name was later shortened to Grand Central, before eventually turning into Champagne, among other, often temporary names. No matter. They decided to throw themselves headlong into music. Prince already had the right kind of name, and Andre later changed his to André—adding a little accent for effect—Cymone. **Nobody knew it at the time, but this wasn't the last the world would hear of them.**

1975 - 1978

THE GIFT OF MUSIC

As early as the mid-1970s, as he was barely entering adulthood, the self-taught musician Prince impressed all those who heard him with his musical intuition and his talents as a multi-instrumentalist. He played the piano like his father John, of course, but also the guitar, the bass, the drums, percussion, and more. He was extraordinarily gifted and mastered up to twenty instruments, not to mention the most important one, perhaps: the techniques and tools of the recording studio.

ART: Samir Dahmani

One night, after a show, I remember seeing a shooting star.

So I made a wish.

PLEASE MAKE IT SO THAT GRAND CENTRAL AND I MAKE IT...

...AND BECOME FAMOUS.

It's cool that my wish came true...

Give or take one small detail.

It didn't come true for me, André Cymone, so much as it did to my best buddy...

...Prince.

THANKS ANYWAY...

YOU CAME CLOSE.

Besides, I couldn't fight it. He had enormous potential and everybody knew it. Every band in town wanted him.

Starting with Pepe Willie, the fiancé of one of Prince's cousins, who was already helping Grand Central get gigs.

He hired him as a guitar player in his band 94 East.

AND I PLAYED FOR THAT BAND TOO, YOU KNOW?

Cool.

But Prince went above and beyond: he played the drums, the keyboard...and ended up writing songs.

"Just Another Sucker," for example...

...is one of his!

Just another Sucker *

"Minneapolis Genius" can be considered Prince's first pro album.**

EVEN THOUGH HE ALWAYS REFUTED THAT IDEA. GO FIGURE.

Talk to us about 1976.

*IT HAS NEVER BEEN CLEARLY ESTABLISHED WHETHER PRINCE COULD OR COULDN'T READ AND WRITE MUSIC.
**IT WAS RELEASED FEBRUARY 12, 1986 ON VINYL THEN ON CD A FEW MONTHS LATER.

1976, THAT'S THE YEAR TO HE HOOKED UP WITH SONNY THOMPSON, THE BASS PLAYER FOR THE FAMILY.

THOSE GUYS SERIOUSLY ROCKED TOGETHER!

AND ACTUALLY, SONNY T LATER JOINED ONE OF PRINCE'S BANDS FROM THE 90S: NEW POWER GENERATION.

SO WAS THAT A PIVOTAL YEAR FOR HIM?

Yep, thanks to a contest, Grand Central won a few free hours at a recording studio.

So we show up at Chris Moon's place, the owner of Moon Sound, to record a demo.

And during our lunch break...

Moon almost choked.

KOF! KOF!

He grabbed him and offered him a deal on the spot!

WRITE MY SONGS AND YOU CAN USE MY STUDIO AS MUCH AS YOU WANT!

NO 15-BUCKS-AN-HOUR FOR YOU, MAN. FREE.

AFTER THAT, HE DIDN'T COME TO REHEARSAL AS MUCH...

HE SPENT ALL HIS TIME AT MOON'S...

...AND EVENTUALLY QUIT THE BAND.

"IF YOU THINK THIS CAN WORK, GO FOR IT, MAN!"

THAT'S WHAT I TOLD HIM!

GRAND CENTRAL, WHICH WE HAD RENAMED CHAMPAGNE...

...STRUGGLED WITHOUT PRINCE...

...AND DISSOLVED IN '78.

SO MUCH FOR OUR DREAMS OF GLORY....

AND HUSNEY, IN ALL THIS?

Ah, Owen Husney... Moon turned him on to Prince in the summer of '76.

CHECK OUT THIS DEMO, OWEN!

His reaction was immediate.

IT'S CRAP!

RELAX, MAN, I'M JUST KIDDING.

YOUR MAN'S AWESOME BUT YOUR TAPE SUCKS.

TELL HIM I'M IN.

HERE'S THE PLAN.

WE DO A NEW, HIGH QUALITY DEMO.

I'LL GET DAVID Z TO DO THE SOUND. HE'S THE BEST THERE IS.

THEN, WE'LL PUT TOGETHER A PRESS KIT...

...AND A MARKETING CAMPAIGN...

...AND GO AFTER THE BIG LABELS.

ME, I HELPED HIM OUT AS MUCH AS I COULD AND I PLAYED WITH HIM ON HIS FIRST GIGS.

THEN I HAD MY OWN LITTLE CAREER, AND--

OK, GREAT, WE'RE DONE HERE.

THE INTERVIEW'S OVER. THANKS ANDRÉ!

THANK YOU, THAT WAS FUN.

OH, YOU'RE HERE?

NICE OF YOU TO STOP BY AND SAY HI...

YEAH, I KNOW.

I LOVE YOU TOO, MAN.

From the very beginning, it was clear that Prince was a born musician. He was never formally trained and he never really learned how to write or decipher a score. And yet he composed and he played intuitively, following his instinct. And his instinct was very good. His relationship with instruments, in particular, would stun all those around him, even at an early age. It was the piano, of course, that first gave him a way to be free. This undoubtedly came from his father. John Nelson, a paradoxical hero who was as intensely admired as he was truly hated, in some cases, remained a model for young Prince. He was the man who "played the best music," as Prince would write much later in his unfinished memoir. Chance had therefore nothing to do with the fact that the keyboard, in its many forms, from the piano to the synthesizer, became his first tool of creation.

But his predilection for instruments didn't stop there. During all his self-taught years in the basement on Russell Avenue, where the mother of his friend Andre Anderson agreed to take him like one of her own children, Prince and Andre set out to learn everything. Guitar, bass, drums, percussion, any and all instruments would do in their efforts to make progress, especially when learning these instruments took the form of a friendly yet very serious competition. Prince dominated those little games, no contest.

Especially so since he began to compose at the same time. Every musician who worked with him from the mid-1970s on immediately grasped the tremendous

Musician and producer Pepe Willie. The first to sense Prince's talent, he recruited him to play on some demos for his band 94 East.

potential of this very young instrumentalist, who was just as comfortable behind the drums or a keyboard as he was holding a guitar neck. Thus Pepe Willie, a musician and aspiring music producer on the Minneapolis music scene, recruited Prince to play guitar on the demos of his band, 94 East, with the potential of more gigs if things worked out. Prince would later say that the band's debut album, *Minneapolis Genius*, which features at least one of his compositions, can actually be considered his first real studio album.

Another one of his buddies from back then, former ad man turned concert promoter

A VORACIOUSLY SELF-TAUGHT ARTIST, THE PROMISING YOUNG MUSICIAN PRINCE WAS ANXIOUS TO LEARN EVERYTHING, MASTER EVERYTHING. AND HE DAZZLED ALL THOSE AROUND HIM WITH THE VIRTUOSIC EASE WITH WHICH HE PLAYED ALL THE INSTRUMENTS.

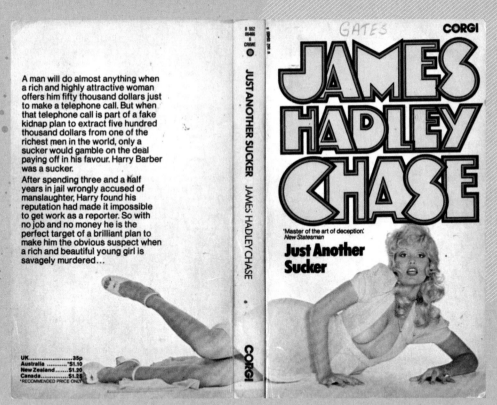

A man will do almost anything when a rich and highly attractive woman offers him fifty thousand dollars just to make a telephone call. But when that telephone call is part of a fake kidnap plan to extract five hundred thousand dollars from one of the richest men in the world, only a sucker would gamble on the deal paying off in his favour. Harry Barber was a sucker.

After spending three and a half years in jail wrongly accused of manslaughter, Harry found his reputation had made it impossible to get work as a reporter. So with no job and no money he is the perfect target of a brilliant plan to make him the obvious suspect when a rich and beautiful young girl is savagely murdered…

UK......................35p
Australia *$1.10
New Zealand.......$1.20
Canada................$1.25
*RECOMMENDED PRICE ONLY

0 552 09466 0 CRIME

JUST ANOTHER SUCKER JAMES HADLEY CHASE

CORGI

GATES CORGI

JAMES HADLEY CHASE

'Master of the art of deception.'
New Statesman

Just Another Sucker

The excellent blog princesongs.org notes the astonishing coincidence between the release date of this crime novel and the release date of the similarly titled track on the 94 East album. Had Prince read it or seen it?

Chris Moon, of British origin, also recalls how he was immediately fascinated by the musical talent of this elf who had appeared out of nowhere. Moon, in close collaboration with local radio station KQRS, had set up a mobile recording studio that he rented out to local musicians or used to record concerts. One day during a Grand Central recording session, while everyone was taking a break after four or five hours of intensive work, Moon caught young Prince, who had remained alone in the studio, fluttering from one instrument to the next with confounding ease. Why complicate things by hiring a whole orchestra, Moon later said, when a single musician, of dizzying versatility, would be enough? Moon was genuinely impressed by what he saw and offered the gifted young man a deal: free access to his studio in exchange for compositions. And even at that early stage, there was already no need for being encumbered by a band, even if it is made up of friends like Grand Central. Prince took the deal, as this gave him free reign to familiarize himself with the tools and techniques of a professional recording studio. **He would go on to use it for the rest of his life.**

1977
MINNEAPOLIS GENIUS , by the band 94 East

1977 - 1978

THE ART OF STANDING YOUR GROUND

In 1976 - 1977, Prince took another step in his quest for fame. Now confident in his abilities as a composer and performer, he had to seduce a record company in order to gain access to the general public. A logical objective, which the young man would nevertheless risk by insisting on total control over his work—at the young age of nineteen and without any musical background. Impossible, right? And yet Prince did it.

ART : Céheu

30

May 1977. Prince and his manager, Owen Husney, have a meeting at Warner headquarters.

YOU'RE YOUNG AND YOU HAVEN'T PROVEN YOURSELF YET! IF THEY SIGN YOU, SAY YES TO WORKING WITH AN EXPERIENCED PRODUCER.

NOPE. I WANT TO RETAIN TOTAL CONTROL OF MY MUSIC. YOU KNOW THAT.

DAMMIT, PRINCE, WARNER IS THE BIG LEAGUES. YOU HAVE TO KEEP A LOW PROFILE THIS TIME!

I'LL SAY IT AGAIN, OWEN: I WANT TO WORK ALONE, WITH OR WITHOUT WARNER. I WILL NOT GO BACK ON THAT DECISION.

IT'S NON-NEGOTIABLE.

Meanwhile, in Warner offices, the boss is ready for them.

WE TESTED HIM IN THE STUDIO. THIS KID IS REALLY GOOD. LET'S HOPE HE'S NOT TOO DEMANDING...

DEMANDING? HA! THIS IS WARNER RECORDS, NOT SOME TWO-BIT NEIGHBORHOOD RECORD SHOP. THE LITTLE GENIUS WILL DO WHAT WE TELL HIM, JUST LIKE EVERYBODY ELSE!

IT'S NON-NEGOTIABLE.

Historians, biographers and fans never really found out what happened behind that door.

CLAC!

But one thing is certain: whatever transpired at that meeting led to the first great mystery in Prince's career.

29

Back then, Warner was a very powerful label with a roster of famous producers.

WHITE WILL PRODUCE YOUR ALBUM.

"White" was Maurice White. The founder and producer of, among others, Earth Wind and Fire.

Any musician would have killed to work with such an icon...

MR. WHITE'S TRADEMARK IS BRASS, WHEREAS I PREFER SYNTHESIZERS, SO WE WOULDN'T BE ON THE SAME PAGE...

But not Prince.

THAT'S A NO. I WANT TO BE IN CHARGE.

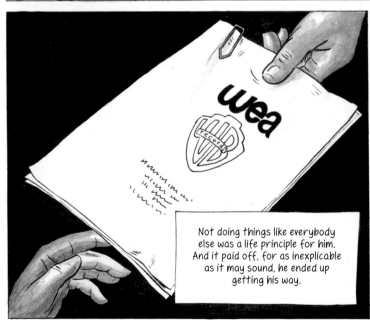

Not doing things like everybody else was a life principle for him. And it paid off, for as inexplicable as it may sound, he ended up getting his way.

Apparently fortune does favor the bold...

Prince signed his first contract in May of 1977: three albums for an advance of 180,000 dollars.

MINNEAPOLIS INTERNATIONAL AIRPORT

He headed for Sausalito, near San Francisco, to record his new album in his new playground, the prestigious Record Plant studio.

He worked on it non-stop from early October to late December 1977.

Warner eventually managed to assign him an executive producer, Tommy Vicari, to oversee the project, as a sort of safeguard.

But Prince ignored him and he just vegetated in the studio, useless.

JUST LIKE STEVIE WONDER: FIRST THE INSTRUMENTS, ONE AT A TIME.

THAT'S HIM THERE, HIDING BEHIND HIS HAVANA.

UM...

...AND THEN WE ADD WITH THE VOCALS.

Just as he had planned, Prince took on all the roles: composer, arranger, songwriter, vocalist and producer.

He played no less than 27 different musical instruments himself to make the album...

...and played parts traditionally reserved for brass and string instruments on the synthesizer, thereby laying the groundwork for the "Minneapolis Sound."

After some overdubbing sessions at the Sound Labs recording studio in Los Angeles in January 1978, he finally finishes his first opus... completely exhausted.

He was an absolute "wreck," as he himself would later say.

Meanwhile, Warner thought that Prince being a one-man-orchestra, that would reduce the cost of hiring a lot of musicians.

SORRY, HOLD ON A SEC.

RiiiING RiiiING

Wrong: recording studio costs had exploded and the budget for all *three* albums was spent on making just the first one!

HOW MUCH?!

A difficult project for all, especially since the album wasn't exactly a hit...

PRINCE-FOR YOU

"For You" had a few beginner's mistakes, true, but nothing for Prince to be ashamed of.

Prince was a diamond in the rough who didn't just suddenly stop shining! He was just molding his brand and patiently cultivating his own legend...

But for all the historians, biographers and fans, the mystery endures: as talented as he was, how did Prince, at such a young age, manage to impose his artistic vision and produce his own album on the dime of a major label?

Don't look for an answer, you'll never find it. Besides... the mystery of it is too beautiful to be tainted by futile suppositions.

By the time the late 70s rolled around, Prince knew what he wanted, without a shadow of a doubt: to compose and to play. Again, everywhere, always. He also knew, with the same determination, what he was capable of: everything. Absolutely everything.

Well, at least that's what it was like on paper. But for that to actually happen, he still had to learn how to convey it to others. And heaven knows that communication was not the first quality that came to mind with regard to this person who barely spoke at all. There was probably a bit of posturing in those extended, if not necessarily calculated, silences. But there was also, unquestionably, in the recesses of the psyche of this highly sensitive soul, a profound sense of reserve, a genuine reluctance to use words. What would be the point, otherwise, of choosing to be a musician?

Be that at his may, he somehow managed to convey his vision to those around him. To wit: by spending all those endless hours in the mobile recording studio that Chris Moon had put at his entire disposal in Minneapolis, the young artist succeeded, over the course of 1976, in producing a fourteen-song demo. The music was his own, of course, but so were the lyrics, which the enterprising Chris Moon encouraged him to write. The main subject was a judicious one: sex, of course. "Puberty hit me with the power of a hurricane," he noted much later in his unfinished memoir, The Beautiful Ones, "and

The cover of the original edition of Prince's unfinished memoir, The Beautiful Ones, written in collaboration with journalist Dan Piepenbring.

from then on, all I could think about was the opposite sex." Prince nevertheless felt that Minneapolis might be too provincial for what he was going for—not to mention that his fellow musicians, who weren't exactly thrilled to see this ambitious man progressing much faster than anyone else, were a bit reticent. Just who the hell did that runt think he was, anyway? Hence the trip to New York that fall, where Prince was determined to let his genius shine before all. It was a little premature on the young man's part, and the plan failed. Faced with such general indifference, he had no choice but to return to his base.

And so it was in Minneapolis, once again,

> **THANKS TO THEIR STUNNING AUDACITY, PRINCE AND HIS FIRST REAL AGENT, OWEN HUSNEY, MANAGED TO ATTRACT INTEREST FROM ONE, TWO, AND THEN THREE MUSIC LABELS. EVEN THOUGH THEY HAD NO TRACK RECORD YET, THEY HAD THE NERVE TO MAKE OUTRAGEOUS DEMANDS... AND IT WORKED!**

that thanks to Chris Moon, he made the other defining connection of this period of his life: Owen Husney, a former musician, publicist and event promoter, who proceeded to make the young man sign an exclusive management contract and promptly promoted himself to the

One of the first checks written by Owen Husney for his protégé. And Prince did indeed endorse it, as evidenced by the signature.

role of Prince's talent agent. While Husney probably wasn't as crafty a fox as many made him out to be, the fact remains that he put Prince on the right track.

He did this by first putting him back to work on new demos--with a chance to reunite with his old friend André Cymone. At the Sound 80 recording studio, where they recorded under the direction of sound engineer David Z., Prince experimented with several models of synthesizers, which he programmed like a brass section, thus

The Warner Music Group, Prince's first record label, was previously called WEA Records for a long time, an acronym for Warner Elektra Atlantic Records.

1978
FOR YOU

developing, by a series of small touches, what would later be called the Minneapolis Sound.

Second, he spun him into a legend, a veritable 007 of music. In the press kit he put together for his little prodigy, Husney deliberately lied about his age. He made him even younger than he was so as to make his precociousness stand out even more. And he really milked Prince's ability to play all the instruments, as if the new kid on the block were a kind of second Stevie Wonder. Suddenly, rumors began to spread, and the whole town was talking about this musical genius from which no one had yet heard a single album.

The strategy worked. Lured by the rumors and the demo, two, and later three big labels made an offer. To which Prince responded with a demand ("intransigence," one might be tempted to call it). In a nutshell: he wanted total creative control. At only nineteen years old and with no track record. No one had ever seen such pretentiousness. Manage everything alone, really?

But it was take it or leave it. Warner took it. Game on.

1979 - 1980

A STAR IS BORN

Now under contract with one of the most powerful record labels in the world, Warner Bros., Prince focuses his activities on two fronts: the album, releasing three of them in a row at the turn of the 1970s and 1980s; and the stage, where he had not really ventured yet. In Minneapolis, audiences at his concerts are blown away by his intensity. And while album sales are still inconsistent, everyone can tell the young prodigy is larger than life.

ART: Christelle Pécout

I HAVE TO ADMIT, *FOR YOU*, WHICH ONLY CAME OUT IN THE U.S., GAVE PRINCE THE OPPORTUNITY TO SHOWCASE HIS IMPRESSIVE CATALOGUE OF TALENTS, WHICH ARE MANY.

HOWEVER, THE RECEPTION WAS LUKEWARM, BY BOTH THE CRITICS AND THE GENERAL AUDIENCE.

THE ALBUM'S TWO SINGLES, "SOFT AND WET," WHICH CAME OUT THE DAY OF HIS 20TH BIRTHDAY, AND "JUST AS LONG AS WE'RE TOGETHER," DIDN'T MANAGE TO REVERSE THAT TREND...

...AND THE ALBUM WAS A COMMERCIAL FLOP.

BUT WHAT NOBODY KNEW AT THE TIME, WAS THAT....

...ON STAGE, DURING HIS BAPTISM BY FIRE...

PETE, YOU GOOD TO GO?

CHECK. TERRY, YOU GOOD?

...PRINCE WOULD TAKE ON A WHOLE OTHER DIMENSION.

WELL, I'M STUCK BEHIND THE MOVING SPOT AND I'M ZONKED, SO LET'S HOPE IT'S NOT A LONG SHOW.

STEVIE WONDER, NO LESS!

...UM...AND NOW, HERE'S THE NEW STEVIE WONDER: PRINCE!

CLAP CLAP

PFFF... FORGET IT. THE GUY LOOKS LIKE HE SMOKED ONE JOINT TOO MANY...

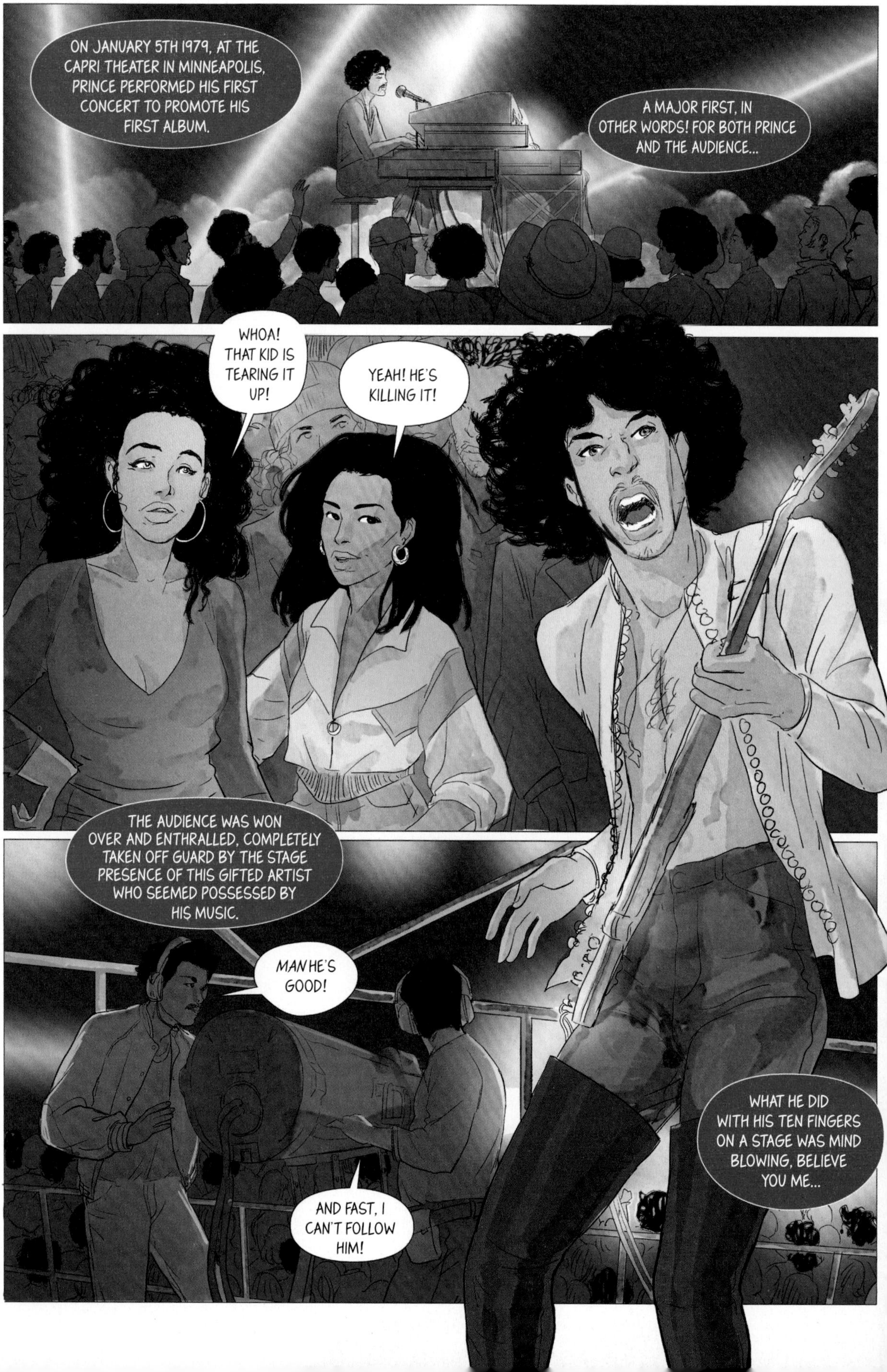
ON JANUARY 5TH 1979, AT THE CAPRI THEATER IN MINNEAPOLIS, PRINCE PERFORMED HIS FIRST CONCERT TO PROMOTE HIS FIRST ALBUM.
A MAJOR FIRST, IN OTHER WORDS! FOR BOTH PRINCE AND THE AUDIENCE...
WHOA! THAT KID IS TEARING IT UP!
YEAH! HE'S KILLING IT!
THE AUDIENCE WAS WON OVER AND ENTHRALLED, COMPLETELY TAKEN OFF GUARD BY THE STAGE PRESENCE OF THIS GIFTED ARTIST WHO SEEMED POSSESSED BY HIS MUSIC.
MAN HE'S GOOD!
AND FAST, I CAN'T FOLLOW HIM!
WHAT HE DID WITH HIS TEN FINGERS ON A STAGE WAS MIND BLOWING, BELIEVE YOU ME...

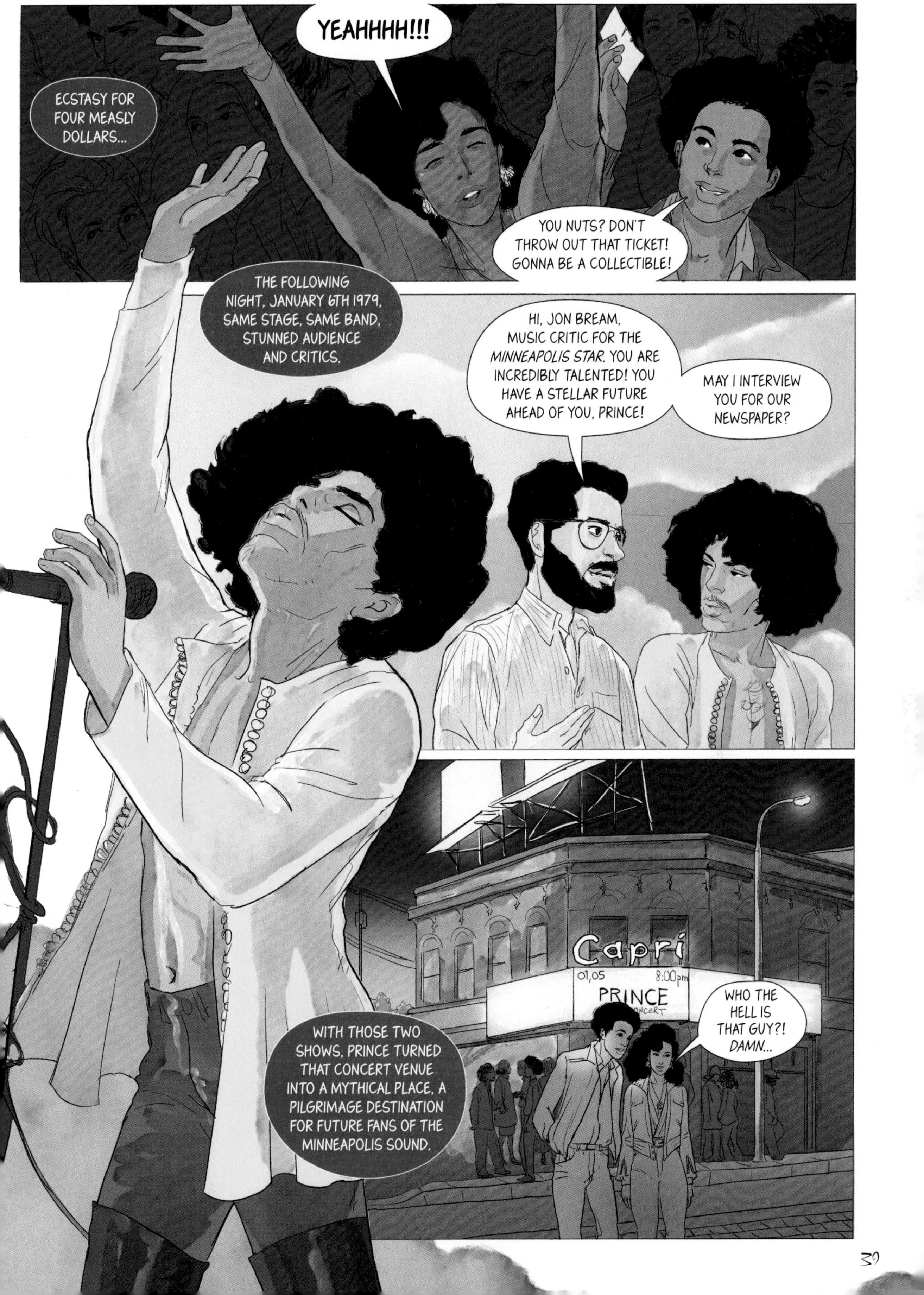
YEAHHHH!!!
ECSTASY FOR FOUR MEASLY DOLLARS...
YOU NUTS? DON'T THROW OUT THAT TICKET! GONNA BE A COLLECTIBLE!
THE FOLLOWING NIGHT, JANUARY 6TH 1979, SAME STAGE, SAME BAND, STUNNED AUDIENCE AND CRITICS.
HI, JON BREAM, MUSIC CRITIC FOR THE *MINNEAPOLIS STAR*. YOU ARE INCREDIBLY TALENTED! YOU HAVE A STELLAR FUTURE AHEAD OF YOU, PRINCE!
MAY I INTERVIEW YOU FOR OUR NEWSPAPER?
Capri
01,05
8:00pm
PRINCE
CONCERT
WHO THE HELL IS THAT GUY?! *DAMN...*
WITH THOSE TWO SHOWS, PRINCE TURNED THAT CONCERT VENUE INTO A MYTHICAL PLACE, A PILGRIMAGE DESTINATION FOR FUTURE FANS OF THE MINNEAPOLIS SOUND.

WHY AM I TELLING YOU ALL THIS? BECAUSE THAT YEAR IS WHEN I, BOB CAVALLO, HAD THE GOOD FORTUNE OF CROSSING PATHS WITH THE PHENOMENON KNOWN AS PRINCE... I STILL REMEMBER THE DAY WE FIRST MET.

FOR WARNER, THE COMMERCIAL FLOP OF THE FIRST ALBUM WAS A STAIN TO BE BLOTTED OUT ASAP: "PRINCE" NEEDED TO RHYME WITH "SUCCESS." AND BINGO: HIS NEXT ALBUM, PRINCE, LESS FINE-TUNED BUT MORE ENERGETIC, WAS THE FIRST ALBUM IN HIS BURGEONING CAREER TO GO PLATINUM!

CAN WE TALK, MR. ARTISTE?

BACK THEN, I WAS WORKING WITH JOSEPH RUFFALO. WE WERE WELL-KNOWN IN THE BIZ, SO WARNER ASKED US TO MANAGE THEIR YOUNG STAR.

YOU'RE INCREDIBLY TALENTED, BUT TRUST ME, YOU REALLY SHOULDN'T WALK OUT ON STAGE IN YOUR UNDERWEAR.

DO YOU KNOW WHAT HE SAID TO THAT?

FINE. STAY FOR THE NEXT SHOW, AND I'LL TAKE THEM OFF FOR YOU!

I WAS ALWAYS IMPRESSED BY HIS SELF-CONFIDENCE. HE PULLED THE SAME STUNT A FEW DAYS LATER.

IF YOU REALLY WANT TO KNOW ME, THEN MOVE TO MINNEAPOLIS.

BUT I... I CAN'T JUST MOVE MY WHOLE FAMILY OUT HERE FROM L.A.!

FIND A SOLUTION.

SO I OFFERED ONE OF MY YOUNG EMPLOYEES, STEVE FARGNOLI, THE FOLLOWING DEAL...

I KNOW YOU HOPE TO MAKE PARTNER IN OUR FIRM. AND YOU WILL, SO LONG AS YOU FOLLOW PRINCE AND MOVE TO MINNEAPOLIS.

HE ACCEPTED, AND OUR DUO BECAME A TRIO.

DESPITE HIS SUCCESS, PRINCE DIDN'T REST ON HIS LAURELS. HE RELEASED *DIRTY MIND* RIGHT AFTER: A REAL ARTISTIC DEPARTURE.

HE FOLLOWED NEW FASHION TRENDS LIKE PUNK OR NEW WAVE AND WORKED HARD TO DEVELOP A MORE PROVOCATIVE PERSONA, BOTH IN TERMS OF HIS LOOKS AND HIS LYRICS.

THE ALBUM WAS RELEASED BECAUSE WE SMOOTHED THINGS OVER WITH WARNER. THEY WENT ALONG WITH IT BUT DIDN'T PROMOTE IT MUCH: THE LYRICS WERE TOO EXPLICIT FOR THOSE DAYS.

THE ALBUM WAS A FLOP.

HOWEVER, EVEN THOUGH IT DIDN'T GET MUCH AIRTIME, IT STILL GOT HEARD: THE NIGHTCLUBS PLAYED THE TRACKS *UPTOWN*, *HEAD*, AND *DIRTY MIND* ALMOST NONSTOP!

AND THEN, A CERTAIN MICK JAGGER HEARD IT AND TOOK AN INTEREST IN OUR YOUNG PROTÉGÉ...

CRITICS AND THE PRESS FOLLOWED SUIT AND, A YEAR AFTER HIS FIRST TV APPEARANCE ON AMERICAN BANDSTAND, THEY FINALLY SAW HIM AS "THE SUCCESSOR OF JIMI HENDRIX AND SLY STONE." IT WAS A DONE DEAL.

BEFORE LONG, PRINCE HAD THE WORLD AT HIS FEET. AND I WAS LUCKY TO WITNESS AND BE A PART OF THE GOLDEN YEARS OF THIS VERITABLE EXTRATERRESTRIAL.

NOW? I'M PEACEFULLY ENJOYING MY OLD AGE. HE WASN'T THAT FORTUNATE...

HE STILL HAD SO MUCH TO GIVE THE WORLD.

41

despite the artist's insolent versatility (composer, arranger, lyricist, singer, producer, multi-instrumentalist), despite the size of the sums invested in him (a 180,000-dollar advance for three albums), despite going way over-budget (the entire advance was consumed immediately), despite the flattering reputation as a prodigy that was lavished upon the young musician... Prince's very first album, *For You*, which was released in April 1978, was not the triumph he had hoped for – not by a long shot. The only consolation: one of the nine tracks on the album, *Soft and Wet*, managed to place 92nd on the Billboard Hot 100, the weekly ranking of the top hundred best-selling singles in the United States. At least there was that. But our hero was not the type to let disappointment bring him down. It didn't work out on the first try? All the more reason to hurry up and produce a second one – especially since the record company, Warner Bros, had contractually committed to it.

> ## A FIRST ALBUM, QUICKLY, THEN A SECOND ONE, EVEN FASTER. AND MEANWHILE, STUNNING STAGE PERFORMANCES THAT ELECTRIFIED AN AWE-STRUCK AUDIENCE. FINALLY, SOMETHING NEW IN MINNEAPOLIS!

And so, Prince immediately launched into the making of a new album. Meanwhile, in order not to lose his momentum, the young artist also focused on a new realm: the stage. It would be a defining moment, as it would help everyone realize that the newcomer was not just a made-in-the-studio musician: he was also an exceptional performer.

The wheels were thus set in motion and Prince's first official concert took place on Friday, January 5, 1979 at 8 p.m. in Minneapolis, at the Capri Theater. Tickets were only 4 dollars. Peanuts, especially given the intensity of what unfolded on stage that evening.

Prince
IN CONCERT
A Benefit Performance for the Capri Theatre

Friday, January 5, 8:00 pm
$4.00 in advance $4.75 at the door
Capri Theatre, 2027 West Broadway

PRINCE

The "historic" ticket for Prince's concert at the Capri Theater in Minneapolis (picture on the left). His performance on stage was like an earthquake: a revelation!

Surrounded by a small group of musicians who for the most part knew him well (namely André Cymone on bass, Dr. Fink on keyboard, Dez Dickerson on guitar, Bobby Z. on drums), Prince put on an incandescent show that night, which would be forever engraved in the memory of all those present. And he went on to repeat the feat the next day in the same venue, which was enough to convince the local media that finally, something new had appeared on the Minneapolis music scene.

From then on, everything was set in motion for good. In the following fall, driven by the very positive buzz generated by his memorable live performances, the release of the second album, simply titled *Prince*, took a much more encouraging turn than the first one had. Then again, the artist, in a burst of inspiration, had the wise idea to inject into much of this album the influences that gave birth to his very specific musical signature: rhythm 'n' blues, funk, and soul, in addition rock and pop; in short, everything that helped develop the imagination of young Prince. This cocktail of sounds hit the mark: one million copies sold, driven in particular by the single I Wanna Be Your Lover.

Prince's star was born. Never to be extinguished again. This was confirmed by a third LP, *Dirty Mind*, launched exactly one year after *Prince*, in October 1980, in the fever of this nascent craze. Even more confident in its stylistic and musical choices, the new album established Prince as an author in his own right. Musically, he further broadened his palette, adding touches of pop and New Wave, the main musical trends at the time, to his funk inspired sound. And in terms of lyrics, he developed what would become, for several years, the matrix of his inspiration: a subtle cocktail of provocation and transgression, against a background of highly sexual imagery. The underwear Prince wears on the cover of *Dirty Mind* set the tone... A form of calculated sexual ambiguity first suggested by the young artist's debut appearance on American TV in January 1980, on *American Bandstand* on ABC. Intensely laconic, if we may be so bold as to use that oxymoron, Prince created a strange atmosphere from the get-go on that show, using knowing half-smiles, allusions and mysterious postures to respond to the host's questions.

The most perceptive observers immediately understood what it was all about: Prince was not only presenting himself as a gifted musician; he was creating a character.

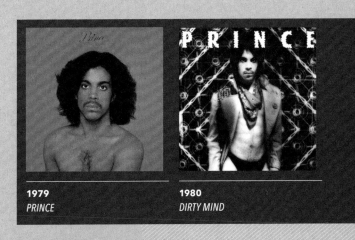

1979
PRINCE

1980
DIRTY MIND

1980 - 1983

SEX, ETC.

By the age of twenty-five, Prince had become both an adult and a pop star. The young musician was fully aware that his power of attraction was closely tied to the sexual ambivalence he displayed. Having come into his own artistically and musically, he was now ready to deliberately amp up the sexual imagery on both his albums and his tours. Prince the provocateur, the embodiment of scandal, would not be easily forgotten...

ART: Joël Alessandra

44

YOU SUCK! GET OFF THE STAGE! BEAT IT!

After seeing him in concert at the Ritz in New York, Mick Jagger invited Prince to open for the legendary Rolling Stones.

The facility was state of the art and close to 100,000 people filled the Los Angeles Memorial Coliseum: October 9, 1981 should have been the best day in his life as a young artist.

It would be his worst nightmare...

WHO THE HELL'S THAT BLACK FAG? WE'RE HERE FOR MICK JAGGER!

BOO! BOO!

Prince had to hurry off the stage after a mere fifteen minutes...

Fans of the Stones, although used to provocative shows, weren't ready for his falsetto and his overtly sexual lyrics. Not to mention his stage outfits: underwear, stocking, trench coat and high heels...

BOOOOO! BOOOOO!

Forty-eight hours later, after Jagger had talked him into a second show, the reception was even more aggressive. Even though he bravely played through his entre set, Prince was booed almost from the get-go.

IF YOU WANT TO BE A HEADLINER, BE PREPARED TO HAVE CANS THROWN AT YOUR FACE. BE PREPARED TO DIE!

What he took away from that incident was that he wasn't sufficiently prepared.

Never again.

45

After that fiasco, Prince had a choice: to either toe the line or keep writing *his* music.

He made his choice by releasing *Controversy* just a few days after that notorious concert, which launched him down the path of his own singularity.

It was funkier and earned him more widespread attention, and laid once and for all the groundwork for the Minneapolis Sound.

Prince's song started getting more airplay and he started headlining at larger venues. His opening act, The Time, was a band started by... Prince himself.

Forever the provocateur, he continued to flirt with sexual ambiguity on *Controversy*: adding to his "Head" and his "Dirty Mind," there was his "Do me Baby" and his "Jack U Off."

He became a sort of sexual icon who projected a transgender image. Black/white, soul/pop, gay/straight...

Prince was always the precursor of the all the hybrid formulas of our time.

While Prince's audience remained primarily black, he took the final step towards his fist real hit with *1999*.

Released just a year after *Controversy*, that album was a real departure in his career.

Prince had only one rule when recording it: total freedom. Unpredictable, bold, out-of-control freedom.

High on sugar, caffeine and David Lynch's strange black and white film *Eraserhead*, he worked on it tirelessly--and alone, even though on stage, he now performed with The Revolution.

With two new toys, an Oberheim synthesizer and a Linn LM-1 rhythm box, he experimented, moving ideas from one composition to the next, shattering the boundaries of format and mixing melodies.

An expert combination of creative whimsy and perfectionism.

The result: the rich double album *1999*, an 11-track orgy in a max version, a punk rocket ship with 11 levels of hits.

A master-piece.

In 1982, the singles "1999," "Little Red Corvette" and "Delirious" gets Prince on the brand new music channel MTV.

Despite Michael Jackson's massive hit *Thriller*, 1999, with its more avant-garde sound, wins the hearts of millions of people.

LITTLE RED CORVETTE BABY, U'RE MUCH 2 FAST

The 1999 Tour was a triumph that broke the record for longest U.S. tour.

PLEASE BE WITH US TONIGHT LORD. IN THE NAME OF JESUS-CHRIST, WE'RE GONNA TEAR THIS UP.

AMEN.

Nicknamed The Triple Threat Tour, it featured three different bands in the same show: The Time, Vanity 6, and Prince and the Revolution.

WOOOH, THEY'RE ON *FIRE* TONIGHT!

MAY GOD PROTECT US...

DON'T WORRY, BAB' GOD IS GREAT, BUT HE AIN'T GONNA STC ME FROM PLAYING THE PIANO ON YOU ASS AND MAKING OI WITH YOU ON STAG!

Just like The Time, Vanity 6 was launched by the star himself. The objective of his opening acts was to really warm up the room: the first one thanks to its joyous funk sound...

YOU'RE UP, GIRLS!

...and the second thanks to its superhot bombshells.

I HAD A BLAST, BOSS!

His satellite bands also helped him reach a wider audience.

There's a moral code to his stage. He's not in disguise there.

In fact, his manager, Steve Fargnoli, often reminded this to the pagans of the "Prince universe": "This is the way he dresses, styles his hair, moves and behaves in everyday life."

"The only difference is that when he's off-stage, he's a lot more mellow!"

HEY! MOVE THE MIC STAND 10 INCHES TO THE RIGHT! NOW!

The days of being booed off the stage in L.A. are now far behind him. Prince dictates his own style.

PRINCE! PRINCE! WE LOVE YOU!

A perfectionist and a control freak, the virtuoso established himself as a unique one-man show, taking stage performance to its highest level of mastery.

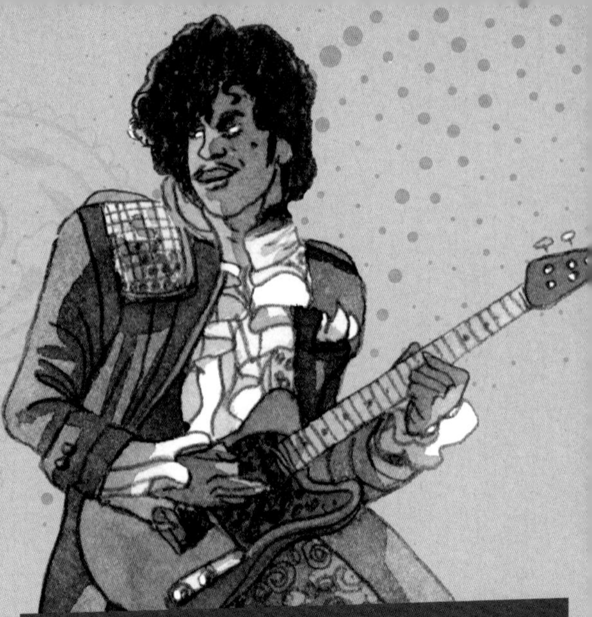

The beginning of the 1980s marked Prince's entry into adulthood, in a way. The trial period was over, it was time to get serious and to embark on a truly unbridled musical and stylistic journey. The young artist manifested his interest in sensuality in all its forms early on. In many ways, music can be used as a very convincing allegory of sex and all its thrills. But along with his entry into maturity, his appetite for the expression of the senses would unfold in all its excess. Even at the cost of a certain level of outrage.

In 1980, the aptly titled *Dirty Mind*, which was one of the top 200 best-selling albums in the U.S. for over six months, had laid the groundwork for a princely inspiration already heavily marked by the passions of the flesh. The lyrics openly refer to fellatio, incest and an immoderate taste for sex in all its forms. Over the following years, Prince would conscientiously lay it on even thicker, even when it meant flirting with transgression.

AFTER SETTING THE GROOVE, IT WAS TIME TO RELEASE THE LIBIDO! PRINCE SET HIS FANS' SENSES ON FIRE WITH THE HELP OF A BAND OF HOT GIRLS IN LINGERIE. AND IF THEY HAPPENED TO OFFEND MEMBERS OF THE AUDIENCE, EVEN BETTER...

During those years, sexual ambiguity was on display at all his performances and openly flaunted. Skimpy underpants, stockings, trench coats and high heels: Prince presented himself as a provocative icon without any taboos, even if it meant being psychologically disturbing to those members in his audience reluctant to be confronted with displays of sexuality. The hostile reception reserved for him, for example, when he opened for the Rolling Stones at a memorable concert in Los Angeles in October 1981, said a lot in this respect. Wait, does this mean that rockers aren't the paragons of tolerance we think they are? Regardless, the Minneapolis Kid, as he was now known, continued to chart his path as a scandalous new star. Trinkets, thongs, rhinestones and sequins, the artist continued to strut on stage with increasingly transgressive postures – and it was clear he was having a ball with it. Especially since, musically speaking, everything was going great, thank you very much. In October 1981, almost a year to the

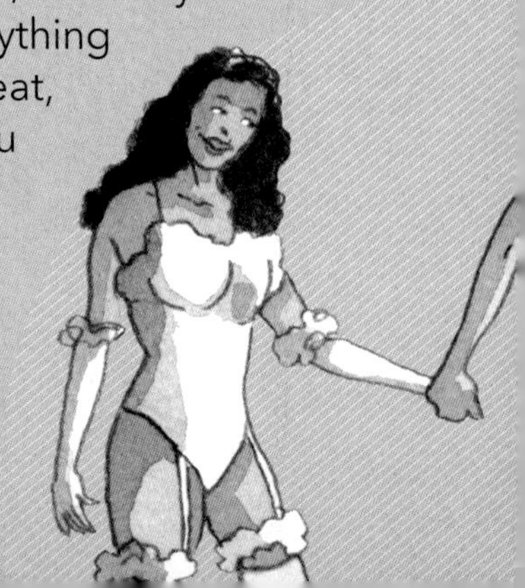

day after his third LP, a new album was released, *Controversy*, which extended and deepened the highly sexual themes and vibes of the previous one. Five hundred thousand copies sold in three months. Prince was now a heavyweight. And even if the relationship between his record company and their notoriously difficult "client" would remain a little tense, Warner had no regrets about the choice they had made back in 1977. Prince immediately followed up the album release with a tour to promote it, the Controversy Tour, while losing himself in what was now his major obsession: non-stop composition and writing. This intensity would result, in October 1982, barely a year after *Controversy*, in the release of his first

1981
CONTROVERSY

1982
1999

double album: *1999*. Permeated with those synthesizers that, one track after another, helped forge the "Minneapolis Sound," the album would bring him both comfortable commercial success (he passed the million-copies-sold mark in just seven months) and his first two major hits, *Little Red Corvette*, which made it into the Top 10, and the title track, *1999*. The lengthy American tour that began in the wake of the double album was a triumph. And its success was reinforced by the emergence of a new player on television screens, the likes of which had never been seen, appearing first in the United States and then soon throughout he world: the music channel MTV, with its music videos played in heavy rotation.. **Prince would soon become one of their headliners.**

After rattling listeners with his albums by unabashedly evoking masturbation, fellatio and incest, Prince applied the same principles to his act on stage, where he just as unabashedly displayed the attributes of unbridled sexuality.

1984
REVOLUTION UNDER A PURPLE RAIN

In less than a decade, Prince has become a name that counts in the world of pop music. But he has yet to win global fame. This will be the goal of his new project, *Purple Rain*, which combines cinema and music for the first time. An intuition that turns out to be determining and elevates the artist to the status of an international superstar, launching him into a new era.

ART: Martin Trystram

Los Angeles
August 1983

CHEERS! I'D SAY BOB AND STEVE AND I DID A HELL OF A JOB TO MAKE YOU A STAR, HUH?

YOU'RE RIGHT, JOE, *1999* WAS A HUGE HIT!

BUT HERE'S THE THING: YOUR CONTRACT WITH CR&F EXPIRES IN A FEW WEEKS, SO WE HAVE TO RENEW IT. HERE, I'VE PRINTED IT OUT. I WON'T BOTHER YOU WITH THE DETAILS. ALL YOU HAVE TO DO IS SIGN.

GO AHEAD, DRINK!

JOE RUFFALO, PRINCE'S MANAGER

IT'S ALL COOL. BUT I HAVE ONE CONDITION.

I WANT A MOVIE!

A MOVIE?

Sluurp

A MOVIE ABOUT ME, PRODUCED BY A BIG STUDIO, WITH MY NAME ABOVE THE TITLE!

OTHERWISE, I'M NOT SIGNING.

ANOTHER TAKE!

CLAP!

FiLM : PURPLE RAiN
PRODUCTiON : WARNER BROS
REAL : ALBERT MAGNOLi
SCENE 8 / # 3
1983

1

CUT!

THAT WAS TERRIBLE! EXCEPT FOR PRINCE, YOU WERE GREAT! BUT EVERYBODY ELSE, WAKE THE HELL UP!

ALL RIGHT. WE'LL BREAK FOR LUNCH NOW AND RESUME LATER.

ALBERT MAGNOLI, THE DIRECTOR

ASIDE FROM PRINCE HIMSELF, NOBODY BELIEVED IN HIS MOVIE. SO TO MAKE HIS DREAM COME TRUE, HE HAD TO FOOT PART OF THE BILL.

As did his managers. "I don't want the movie funded by drug dealers or some stupid jeweler."

CAN I GET A REAL COCKTAIL? I'M SICK OF THIS TASTELESS COLORED WATER.

HEY CUTIE PIE, WANNA HAVE LUNCH WITH ME TODAY?

BRAVO! YOU WERE GREAT!

THANKS, JOE.

NOT LIKE THAT OTHER LOSER.

JUST BETWEEN US... WHY'D THEY PICK THAT GUY TO PLAY ME? I'M NOT *THAT* UGLY!

UM...

ANYWAY, LISTEN. WE HAVE A REAL PROBLEM WITH THE DIRECTOR!

HE DOESN'T LIKE ANY OF THE 100 SONGS YOU SUGGESTED FOR THE CLIMACTIC SCENE!

RELAX, JOE. I'M SINGING A FEW NEW SONGS TONIGHT. BY THE END OF THE SHOW, I'LL HAVE FOUND WHAT HE WANTS.

It was on that 3rd day in August 1983, on First Avenue, that for the first time, Prince performed...

PURPLE RAIN PURPLE RAAAiiiN

AMAZING! IT'S IN THE CAN!

YES, BOSS.

THAT GAVE ME THE GODDAMMED CHILLS!

3

*WORDS PRINCE TOLD HIS FRIEND PATRICE RUSHER, A SINGER AND PIANIST.

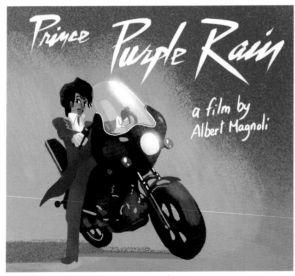

July 26, 1984, Mann's Chinese Theater. The period of anxiety leading up to the release of *Purple Rain*, probably the only one in his career, paled in comparison...

...to the pride he felt that night.

A flamboyant, egomaniacal trip, *Purple Rain* was an incredible exercise in pop self-celebration of Prince by Prince himself.

The landslide the star predicted did take place. The Grammies, the Oscars...he won a bunch of awards!

As he had also predicted, *Purple Rain* changed his life.

The album turned Prince into a king. As for the film, it added one more jewel to his crown.

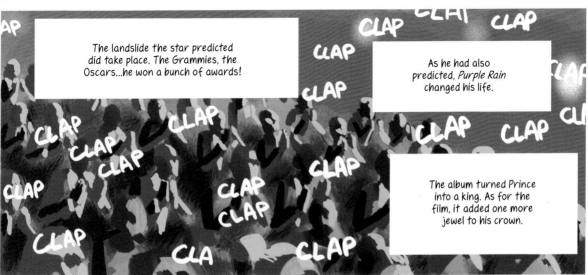

Tryptram + Lourenco   5

The lives and careers of musicians are often arranged around a pivotal moment, a turning point from which everything changes to enter a new era. A key song often acts as the trigger. Neil Young and *Harvest*. Led Zeppelin and *Stairway to Heaven*. AC/DC and *Highway to Hell*. David Bowie and his appearance on Top of the Pops. That kind of thing. For Prince, the year where everything truly changed was 1984. The year *Purple Rain* was released.

The birth of this defining project can be pinpointed to the time when Prince was preparing the 1999 double album. The artist was (already) feeling the need to reinvent himself, as would be the case on many occasions throughout his very prolific career. You have to offer something new, display something new. Innovation would take the form of the new band that would henceforth accompany him on his journey. He called this band The Revolution. In actuality, for anyone relatively familiar with Prince's journey up until then, the band's newness was relative. The Revolution

brought together many of the very reliable musicians who had known and performed with the singer for years, such as Gayle Chapman, André Cymone, Bobby Z. and Doctor Fink. But there were also a few new faces his fans hadn't seen yet, such as guitarist Wendy Melvoin, who took over from Dez Dickerson after he left in search of new adventures, and Lisa Coleman, with whom she would later form the duo Wendy and Lisa.

The poster for *Purple Rain*, the movie. It received a triumphant welcome in the U.S. but went almost unnoticed in Europe.

The changes didn't stop there, of course. What Prince was looking for was to make an impression, a big splash. His major discovery would consist in combining an album project and a film project, the former being the soundtrack for the second. The narrative framework of the feature film didn't bother much with fiction: Purple Rain was essentially a transposition, a just barely fictionalized biography of Prince himself, against a backdrop of family problems and competition between rival bands. After Hollywood and Warner turned their nose down at the project, Prince's

> **A MASSIVE INTERNATIONAL HIT IN LESS THAN TEN DAYS FROM ITS RELEASE! BY COMBINING AN ALBUM, A FILM, AND FLAWLESS INSPIRATION, PRINCE FOUND THE WINNING FORMULA TO CONQUER THE WORLD.**

Purple Rain

In London in February 1985, Prince won the Best International Artist and Best Film awards for *Purple Rain* at a TV awards show..

producers and managers (Owen Husney, his artistic agent in the early days, had been dismissed some time earlier and replaced by Steven Fargnoli) produced the film. It was shot in November 1983, mainly in Minneapolis and in particular at the First Avenue nightclub for the stage parts, and directed by Albert Magnoli.

Bad move on the part of the Hollywood bigwigs: Purple Rain was released in U.S. theaters at the end of July 1984 and became an instant box office hit, earning back its seven million dollar production budget in just three days. All told, it would in bring in more than seventy-one million dollars. And the album of the same name, which was released a month earlier and was masterful in the way it synthesized funk, rock, rhythm 'n' blues and even electronics, had an even more impressive run. Over the long term, it sold more than twenty-two million copies worldwide, including thirteen million in the U.S. alone.

In addition to the track *Purple Rain* itself, which has since become an anthem of global pop music, two hits boosted the album's popularity, *Let's Go Crazy* and *When Doves Cry*. The tour that followed, the Purple Rain Tour, was also a colossal success, selling around 1.7 million tickets. Last but not least, there were the awards: Oscar for best film music in 1985, two Grammy Awards and three American Music Awards the same year. **Enough, already**

1984
PURPLE RAIN

1985 - 1989

JAMMIN' WITH SHEILA

In the mid-1980s, now firmly established in the firmament of musical notoriety, Prince entered the most fruitful period of his artistic journey. This creativity also draws from an extraordinarily stimulating environment, where women, central to his inspiration, have a tremendous influence. For a few years, one of them, the percussionist Sheila E., will play a decisive role alongside her mentor, both on and off stage.

ART: Samuel Figuière

USA – 1991!

AAAAAARGLL

I... CAN'T... BREATHE...

CALM DOWN, MA'AM, CALM DOWN!

KOF! KOF! ARGLLL

HOLD HER DOWN!

YOU'LL BE OK, MRS. ESCOVADO. LIE DOWN.

THINK OF SOMETHING PLEASANT. YOUR FAMILY, YOUR FRIENDS...

YOUR BOYFRIEND, MAYBE?

PHOOPH! HNNN! MY... BOYF...

YES... I REMEMBER....

I REMEMBER THE MOMENT...

...I MET HIM...

1981, WE HAD CROSSED PATHS THREE YEARS EARLIER, ON TOUR, BUT OF COURSE...

...YOU PRETENDED YOU DIDN'T REMEMBER.

DAMN! YOU GOT SKILLS, BABY!

OH, MUSIC RUNS IN MY FAMILY, SO, YOU KNOW...

OH YEAH?

MY DAD PLAYS THE LATIN PERCUSSION FOR TITO PUENTE.

AND MY UNCLE COKE'S BEEN WITH CARLOS SANTANA FOR AGES.

AND WHAT ABOUT YOU?

I'VE WORKED WITH LIONEL RICHIE, MARVIN GAYE, HERBIE HANCOCK, DIANA ROSS, AND THESE DAYS I PLAY WITH GEORGE DUKE.

COOL!

YOU'RE THE KIND OF GIRL I WANT IN MY BAND. BUT I'M BETTING I CAN'T AFFORD YOU.

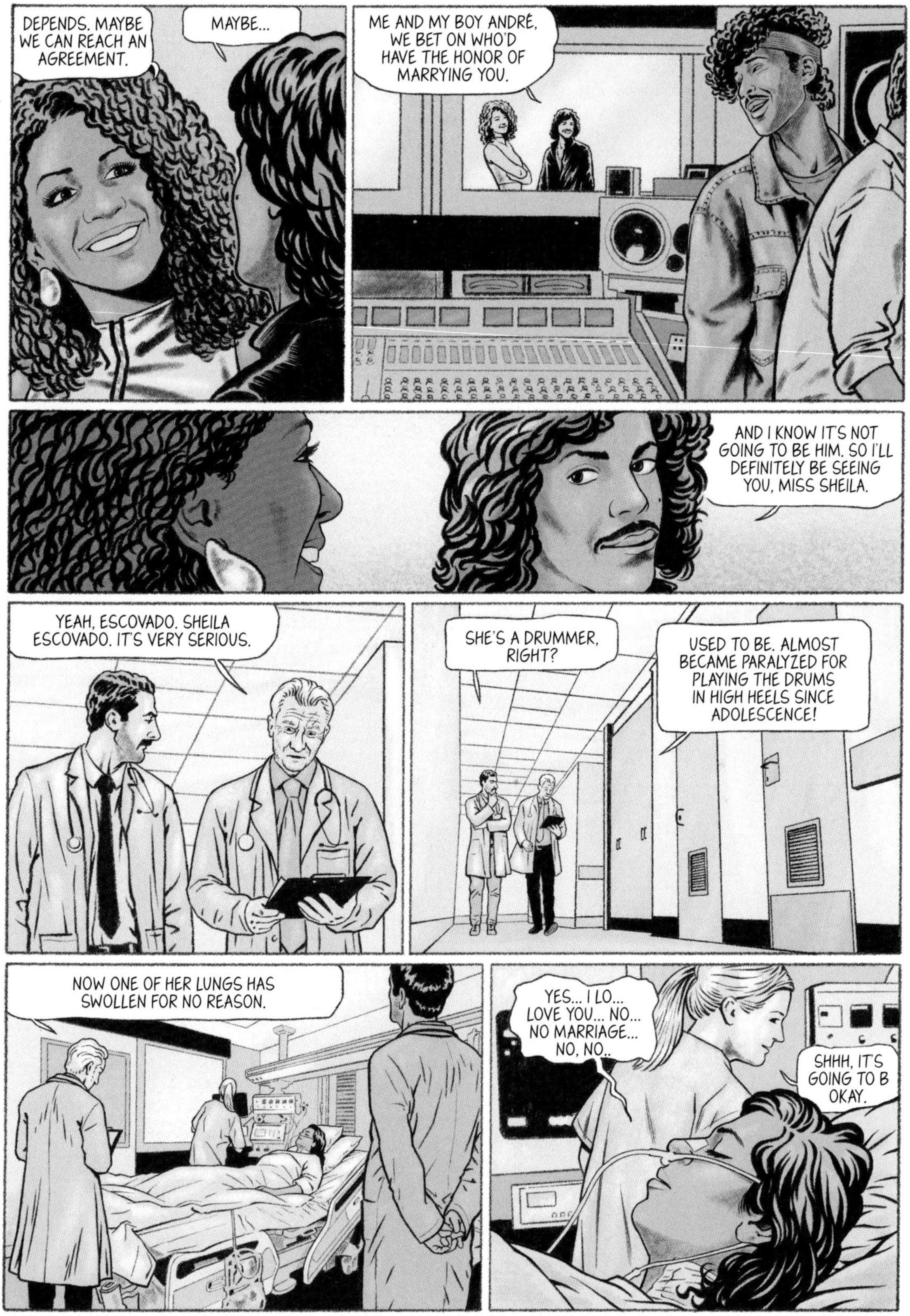
DEPENDS. MAYBE WE CAN REACH AN AGREEMENT.
MAYBE...
ME AND MY BOY ANDRÉ, WE BET ON WHO'D HAVE THE HONOR OF MARRYING YOU.
AND I KNOW IT'S NOT GOING TO BE HIM. SO I'LL DEFINITELY BE SEEING YOU, MISS SHEILA.
YEAH, ESCOVADO. SHEILA ESCOVADO. IT'S VERY SERIOUS.
SHE'S A DRUMMER, RIGHT?
USED TO BE. ALMOST BECAME PARALYZED FOR PLAYING THE DRUMS IN HIGH HEELS SINCE ADOLESCENCE!
NOW ONE OF HER LUNGS HAS SWOLLEN FOR NO REASON.
YES... I LO... LOVE YOU... NO... NO MARRIAGE... NO, NO..
SHHH, IT'S GOING TO B OKAY.

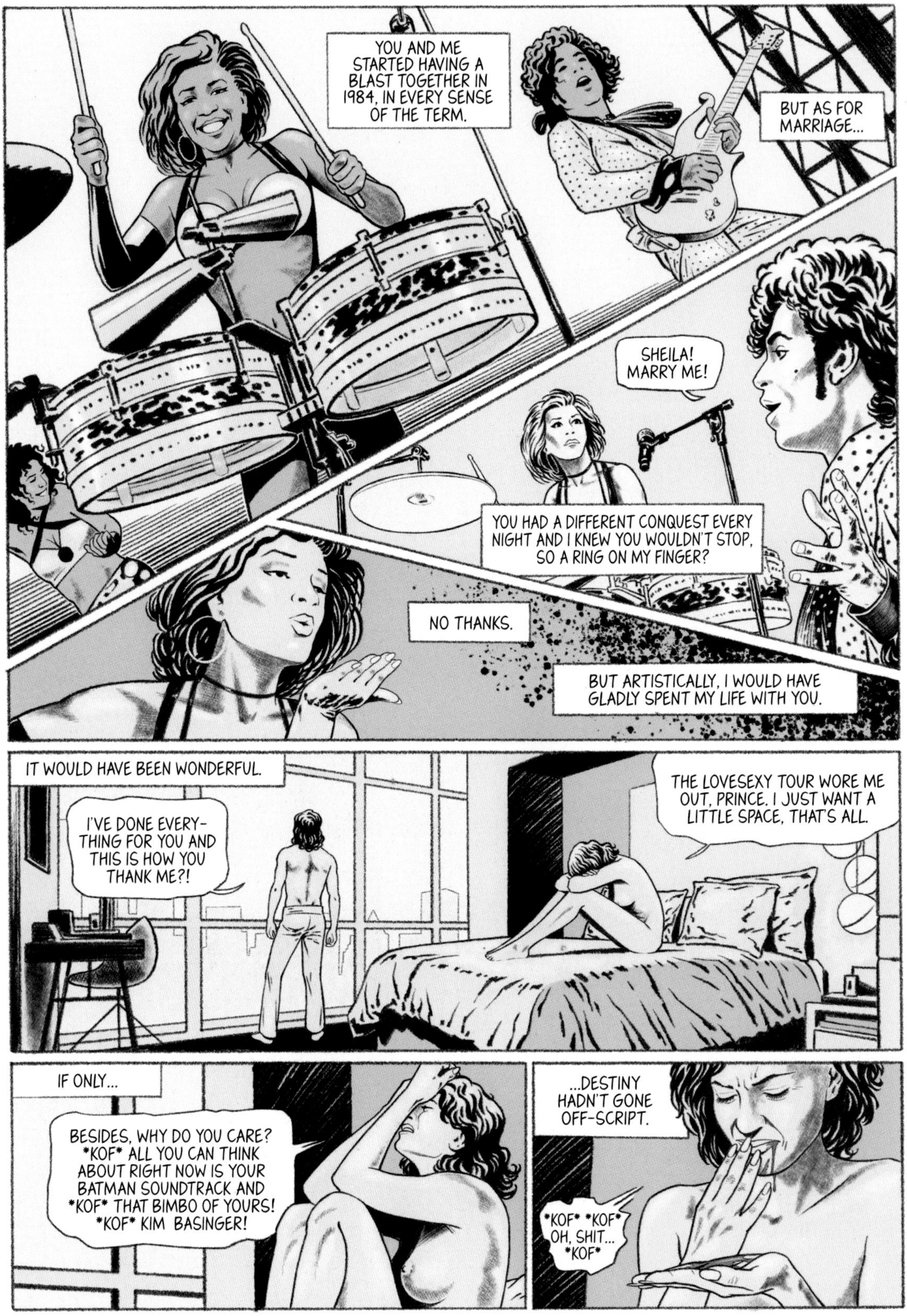
YOU AND ME STARTED HAVING A BLAST TOGETHER IN 1984, IN EVERY SENSE OF THE TERM.
BUT AS FOR MARRIAGE...
SHEILA! MARRY ME!
YOU HAD A DIFFERENT CONQUEST EVERY NIGHT AND I KNEW YOU WOULDN'T STOP, SO A RING ON MY FINGER?
NO THANKS.
BUT ARTISTICALLY, I WOULD HAVE GLADLY SPENT MY LIFE WITH YOU.
IT WOULD HAVE BEEN WONDERFUL.
I'VE DONE EVERYTHING FOR YOU AND THIS IS HOW YOU THANK ME?!
THE LOVESEXY TOUR WORE ME OUT, PRINCE. I JUST WANT A LITTLE SPACE, THAT'S ALL.
IF ONLY...
BESIDES, WHY DO YOU CARE? *KOF* ALL YOU CAN THINK ABOUT RIGHT NOW IS YOUR BATMAN SOUNDTRACK AND *KOF* THAT BIMBO OF YOURS! *KOF* KIM BASINGER!
...DESTINY HADN'T GONE OFF-SCRIPT.
KOF *KOF* OH, SHIT... *KOF*

NOW LOOK HOW I ENDED UP.

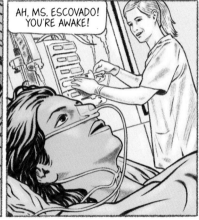

AH, MS. ESCOVADO! YOU'RE AWAKE!

AFTER THAT HEALTH SCARE, SHEILA E. WENT ON WITH HER LIFE AND HER SOLO CAREER.

IN THE EARLY 2000S, SHE PERIODICALLY JOINED PRINCE ON TOUR.

IT WAS MUTUAL, IRRESISTIBLE ATTRACTION.

SOME FANS, THE PURISTS, RESENTED HER FOR HER ABSENCES AND, IN THEIR VIEW, FOR TAKING ADVANTAGE OF THE STAR.

BE THAT AS IT MAY, SHEILA E. SHARED PRINCE'S LIFE AND RECORDED THREE ALBUMS ON HIS LABEL. ADDITIONALLY, SHE FOUND TALENTED MUSICIANS FOR HIM WHO ALSO CONTRIBUTED TO THE EVOLUTION OF HIS MUSIC.

WHICH MAKES HER, INDISPUTABLY, ONE OF THE STARS WHO MATTERED IN THE PRINCE GALAXY.

There would be enough material to write ten books about Prince and the women in his life. Many pages of his unfinished autobiography *The Beautiful Ones*, co-written with Dan Piepenbring, are devoted to them. For instance, there was his high school sweetheart Debbie –her last name was not revealed– a cheerleader who turned his senses upside down; Petey, about whom he daydreamed in college; Marcie, the girl from North Minneapolis, who moved him with her slight speech impediment; and Cari, a girl from the projects, whom he portrays in the book as his "first real girlfriend," also writing about the "ridiculously short" skirts she wore all the time: "Cari's body was a call to crime and her natural curves proved to be particularly formidable on weekends." In a more mature form, after his career took off, in the early 80s there would also be Vanity – whose real name was Denise Matthews– a Canadian model and singer whom he made the face of Vanity 6, a band of three women that he supported and who performed songs with ultra-sexualized themes on stage while wearing lingerie. A tantalizing muse made for the screen, Vanity was on the shortlist to play the leading female role in the film *Purple Rain*, but in the end, it was Patricia Kotero, another former cheerleader, who landed the role under the name of Appolonia.

Beyond these more or less fleeting conquests, it was with a "real" musician that Prince would first experience what bore some resemblance to a true love story. California native Sheila Escovedo was born into the music word. Her father and uncle, both professional percussionists, played with prominent artists such as Santana and Tito Puente. It was therefore only natural for her to follow the same path, under the stage name of Sheila E., alongside big names such as George Duke and Marvin Gaye. Recruited to perform for the recording of a track with Prince in 1984, she was immediately noticed by the master, both for her qualities as an instrumentalist and for her, um... flattering figure. And the attraction was clearly mutual. Prince wanted to make Sheila a singer, but she was reluctant. He then had her record what appeared to be background vocals,

A few tickets from Prince's concerts in the mid-1980s.

then cut out his own voice to leave only Sheila as the main vocalist... This time the young beauty was won over. From that moment on, Sheila E. would become a key figure in Prince's life, both on and off the stage. In public, her stage presence was electric and her drum solos would become moments the fans always eagerly anticipated. Prince even asked her to marry him in the middle of a concert once—but in hindsight, it's impossible to say if this was a genuine impulse or simply a gimmick to attract a little media attention.

Sheila left the great Prince circus in 1989, after it became obvious, starting with the recording of the *Batman* soundtrack, that her mentor's focus was elsewhere. But she would nevertheless continue to occupy a very special place in his environment and would periodically reappear alongside him on an album or on stage as a guest artist. **It was as if those two were simply unable to turn the page and forget about their shared history.**

1985
AROUND THE WORLD IN A DAY

1986
PARADE

1986 - 1987

PAISLEY PARK

A global triumph, a magnetic aura, boundless creativity, conquests galore... The only thing Prince is lacking, as the 1980s come to a close, is a personal kingdom over which to reign, far away from the producers and record companies he abhors. This kingdom would be Paisley Park, the complex he had built on the outskirts of Minneapolis with the fortune amassed thanks to Purple Rain.

ART : Baudouin Forget

THE ARCHITECTS FROM BOTO DESIGN DID A FANTASTIC JOB. CONGRATULATIONS, MR. THOENY, THE BOSS IS GOING TO LOVE IT!

I WOULD BE HONORED. BUT PLEASE, CALL ME BRET.

MMM... ARE YOU SURE YOU CAN FINISH ON SCHEDULE, BRET?

I DON'T DOUBT THAT FOR A SECOND. BOSSARDI-CHRISTENSON HAS AN EXCELLENT REPUTATION IN THE CONSTRUCTION INDUSTRY HERE.

BESIDES, THIS PROJECT IS GREAT FOR THE LOCAL ECONOMY!

YOU DON'T REALIZE HOW LUCKY YOU ARE, JEFFREY!

YOU CALL THIS LUCK? DOING EIGHT-HOUR SHIFTS ON A CONSTRUCTION SITE IN THE BURBS?

IT AIN'T JUST ANY CONSTRUCTION SITE, FOOL...

A TEMPLE OF MUSICAL CREATION!

WE'RE BUILDING A TEMPLE, DON'T YOU SEE?

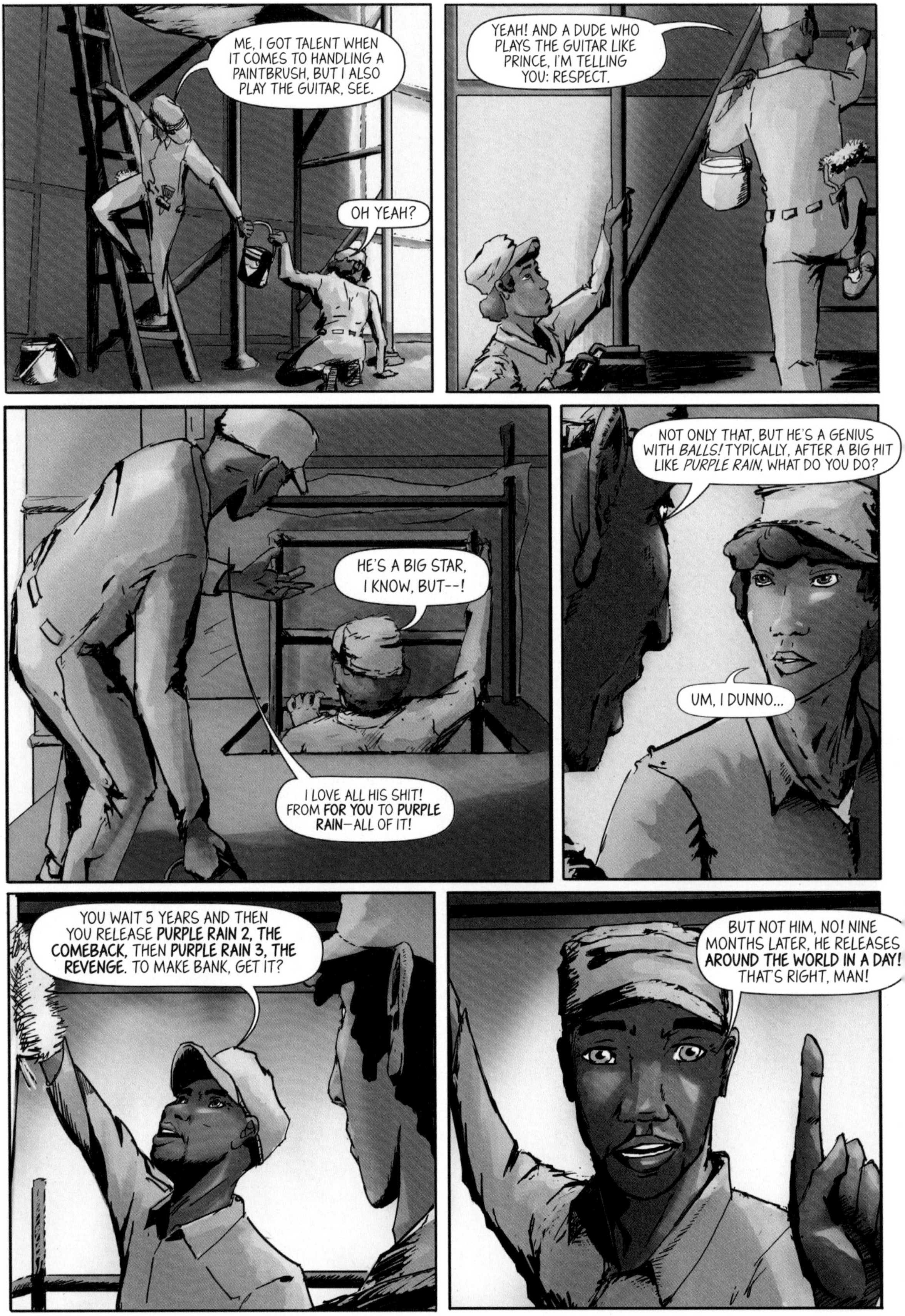

ME, I GOT TALENT WHEN IT COMES TO HANDLING A PAINTBRUSH, BUT I ALSO PLAY THE GUITAR, SEE.
OH YEAH?
YEAH! AND A DUDE WHO PLAYS THE GUITAR LIKE PRINCE, I'M TELLING YOU: RESPECT.
HE'S A BIG STAR, I KNOW, BUT--!
I LOVE ALL HIS SHIT! FROM **FOR YOU** TO **PURPLE RAIN**—ALL OF IT!
NOT ONLY THAT, BUT HE'S A GENIUS WITH *BALLS!* TYPICALLY, AFTER A BIG HIT LIKE *PURPLE RAIN*, WHAT DO YOU DO?
UM, I DUNNO...
YOU WAIT 5 YEARS AND THEN YOU RELEASE **PURPLE RAIN 2, THE COMEBACK**, THEN **PURPLE RAIN 3, THE REVENGE**. TO MAKE BANK, GET IT?
BUT NOT HIM, NO! NINE MONTHS LATER, HE RELEASES **AROUND THE WORLD IN A DAY!** THAT'S RIGHT, MAN!

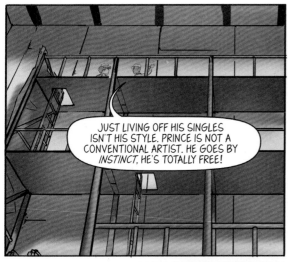

JUST LIVING OFF HIS SINGLES ISN'T HIS STYLE. PRINCE IS NOT A CONVENTIONAL ARTIST. HE GOES BY *INSTINCT*, HE'S TOTALLY FREE!

HE WANTS TO LIVE HIS DREAM AND NOT BE A SLAVE TO OBJECTIVES. YOU FEEL ME?

SO HE INVESTED ALL HIS MONEY INTO THIS PLACE DEVOTED TO MUSIC, IN HIS HOMETOWN OF MINNEAPOLIS!

MEH, HE JUST CRAVES RECOGNITION, LIKE ALL ARTISTS.

MAYBE ON SOME LEVEL, SURE. BUT NOT TO THE POINT OF PROSTITUTING HIMSELF LIKE JACKSON AND OTHERS!

PHIL...?

I'VE SEEN HIM IN CONCERT, THE DUDE CAN PLAY--

PHIL!

WHAT? WHAT'S WRONG?

HOLY SHIT!

71

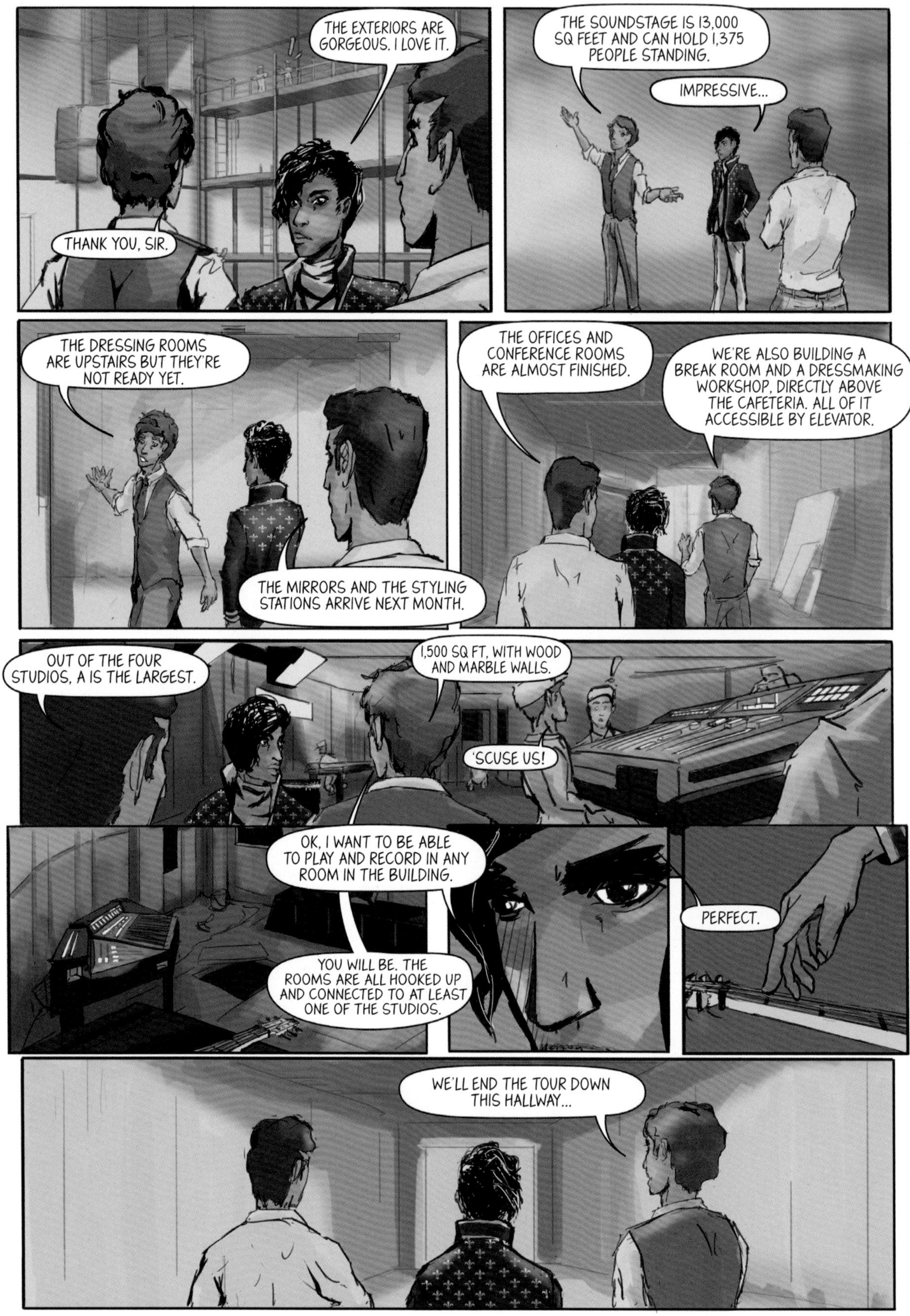
THE EXTERIORS ARE GORGEOUS. I LOVE IT.
THANK YOU, SIR.
THE SOUNDSTAGE IS 13,000 SQ FEET AND CAN HOLD 1,375 PEOPLE STANDING.
IMPRESSIVE...
THE DRESSING ROOMS ARE UPSTAIRS BUT THEY'RE NOT READY YET.
THE MIRRORS AND THE STYLING STATIONS ARRIVE NEXT MONTH.
THE OFFICES AND CONFERENCE ROOMS ARE ALMOST FINISHED.
WE'RE ALSO BUILDING A BREAK ROOM AND A DRESSMAKING WORKSHOP, DIRECTLY ABOVE THE CAFETERIA. ALL OF IT ACCESSIBLE BY ELEVATOR.
OUT OF THE FOUR STUDIOS, A IS THE LARGEST.
1,500 SQ FT, WITH WOOD AND MARBLE WALLS.
'SCUSE US!
OK, I WANT TO BE ABLE TO PLAY AND RECORD IN ANY ROOM IN THE BUILDING.
YOU WILL BE. THE ROOMS ARE ALL HOOKED UP AND CONNECTED TO AT LEAST ONE OF THE STUDIOS.
PERFECT.
WE'LL END THE TOUR DOWN THIS HALLWAY...

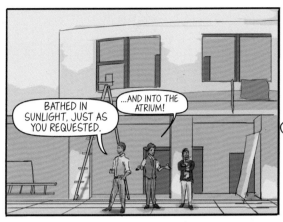

BATHED IN SUNLIGHT, JUST AS YOU REQUESTED.

...AND INTO THE ATRIUM!

GOOD WORK, GUYS. ALL WE NEED NOW IS TO FIGURE OUT WHERE TO HANG THE CAGES OF DIVINITY AND MAJESTY.

THOSE ARE THE BOSS'S DOVES.

HOLY CR--

HI.

HI.

H... HEL... HELLO.

SAVE TWO TICKETS TO THE INAUGURAL CONCERT FOR THOSE GENTLEMEN.

OUTSIDE HIS MUSIC, PAISLEY PARK WAS PRINCE'S MOST EMBLEMATIC PROJECT.

ATTENDING A CONCERT IN THE MASTER'S SANCTUARY WAS A SPECIAL MOMENT FOR HIS FANS.

WELL, FOOL...

LIKE A JOURNEY TO A HOLY LAND.

...WAS THE GIG WORTH IT? HUH?

YEAAAH!

PRINCE! PRINCE! PRINCE!

Paisley Park was almost as much the culmination of a psychological adventure as that of a musical or architectural journey. Paisley Park was the culmination of an almost frenzied quest for independence and omnipotence; Paisley Park, in many ways, was Peter Pan in his realm.

Prince had dreamed of a place like that for so long. A place that would come into being through his inspiration, a place where he would be the master, the magician, the sorcerer – and on which he could count to keep at bay all those whose desires for control or influence he had always fiercely rejected. In 1986, in Chanhassen, about twenty-five miles southwest of Minneapolis, thanks to the enormous income generated by the success of the *Purple Rain* film, album and tour, Prince started to build what was effectively an enormous complex of recording studios, rehearsal rooms and auditoriums, not to mention a private residence – literally an entire domain. This would be his territory, his enchanted stronghold.

> **PRINCE'S KINGDOM HAD A NAME: IT WAS CALLED PAISLEY PARK. BUILT IN THE SUBURBS OF MINNEAPOLIS, THIS HIGH-TECH MUSICAL COMPLEX WOULD BE HIS HIDEOUT AND HIS REFUGE. TODAY, IT'S ONE OF THE KEY STOPS FOR FANS ON A PRINCE PILGRIMAGE.**

He called it Paisley Park, in reference to a song from his 1985 album *Around the World in a Day*, which itself was inspired by the fabrics adorned with a teardrop-shaped floral motif that came from Iran via India, the Paisley or cashmere pattern, which was very fashionable in the textile industry starting in the 19th century and which became trendy again in the 1960s thanks to psychedelia and hippies.

Nothing psychedelic, however, about the lines of the large complex entirely covered in white slabs and designed by the California architectural firm Boto Design, then headed up by Bret Thoeny. One would instead be reminded of a pharmaceutical laboratory or an office complex. It was inside that the atmosphere and the decorations were more... princely. Both the colors and the decor, sometimes baroque, were clearly designed to seduce and dazzle visitors – all in accordance with the personal tastes of the master of the place. To impress, in essence. "A cross between Abbey Road for its cutting-edge technology and Graceland for its flashy kitsch," as a couple of critics once jokingly

Paisley Park today. Behind these almost anonymous façades sits Prince's musical kingdom.

The main atrium of the Paisley Park complex. After Prince's death, the place was converted into a space that celebrates his memory. Respect.

wrote. We could add another, not entirely irrelevant comparison, by mentioning the Neverland complex that Michael Jackson built in California for his own personal use. A Northern Kingdom, in other words.

Four recording studios, rehearsal spaces and music video sets, costume design workshops, luxurious dressing rooms... the technical resources of Paisley Park were impressive. The imposing 13,000 sq ft concert hall alone could accommodate nearly 1400 standing people. Such luxurious facilities of course immediately attracted fans by the thousands, not to mention many renowned artists who were eager to record on site to benefit from Prince's hyper positive aura at that time. And that tradition continues to this day: just recently, in February 2020, the American soul artist Meshell Ndegeocello kicked off a live residency there entitled the Musicology 2020 Concert Series.

After nearly two years of construction, the complex officially opened at 7801 Audubon Road on September 11, 1987, although Prince had actually recorded there the previous April. Several sequences of the film *Sign O' The Times* were also shot there during the summer of that year.

Then Governor of Minnesota Rudy Perpiech himself attended the inauguration and went on to officially call that day "Prince Day..." And indeed the kingdom of the brilliant leprechaun deserved at least that.

1987
SIGN O' THE TIMES

1987 - 1988

RECOGNITION:
SIGN O' THE TIMES

By the mid-1980s, what could Prince possibly still be missing? Perhaps an even deeper artistic aura, an achievement that deserves the qualifier that so many artists are nevertheless wary of: a masterpiece. Without really looking for it, this was the album that Prince released at the beginning of 1987. A definitive album, visionary, unsurpassable, a titanic creation: a double album titled *Sign O' the Times*.

ART: Yvan Ojo

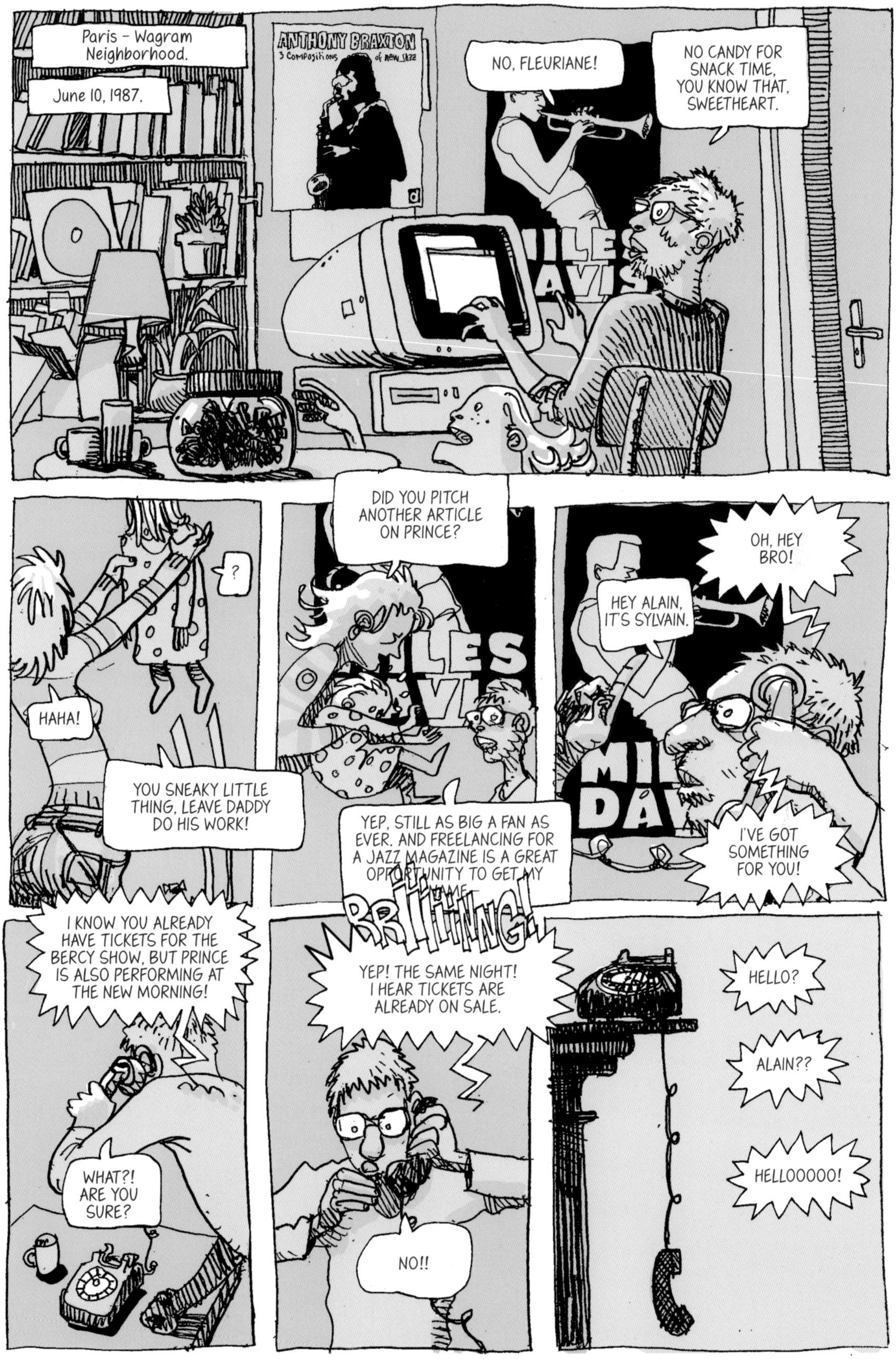

Paris - Wagram Neighborhood.
June 10, 1987.
ANTHONY BRAXTON
3 Compositions of new jazz
NO, FLEURIANE!
NO CANDY FOR SNACK TIME, YOU KNOW THAT, SWEETHEART.
?
HAHA!
YOU SNEAKY LITTLE THING, LEAVE DADDY DO HIS WORK!
DID YOU PITCH ANOTHER ARTICLE ON PRINCE?
YEP, STILL AS BIG A FAN AS EVER. AND FREELANCING FOR A JAZZ MAGAZINE IS A GREAT OPPORTUNITY TO GET MY NAME
BRIIIIIINNG!
HEY ALAIN, IT'S SYLVAIN.
OH, HEY BRO!
I'VE GOT SOMETHING FOR YOU!
I KNOW YOU ALREADY HAVE TICKETS FOR THE BERCY SHOW, BUT PRINCE IS ALSO PERFORMING AT THE NEW MORNING!
WHAT?! ARE YOU SURE?
YEP! THE SAME NIGHT! I HEAR TICKETS ARE ALREADY ON SALE.
NO!!
HELLO?
ALAIN??
HELLOOOOO!

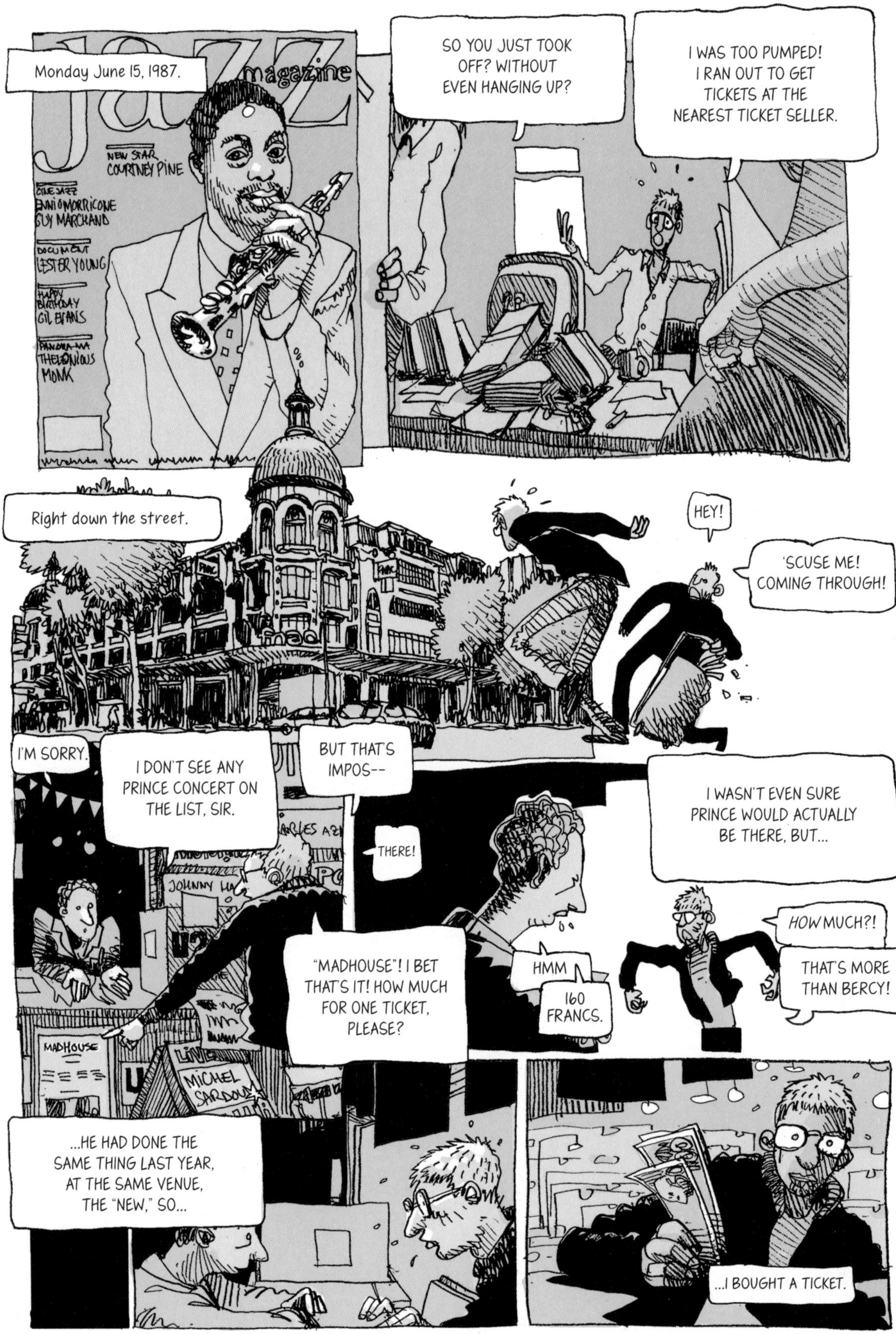
Monday June 15, 1987.
jazz magazine
NEW STAR COURTNEY PINE
CINE JAZZ ENNIO MORRICONE GUY MARCHAND
DOCUMENT LESTER YOUNG
HAPPY BIRTHDAY GIL EVANS
PANORAMA THELONIOUS MONK
SO YOU JUST TOOK OFF? WITHOUT EVEN HANGING UP?
I WAS TOO PUMPED! I RAN OUT TO GET TICKETS AT THE NEAREST TICKET SELLER.
Right down the street.
fnac
HEY!
'SCUSE ME! COMING THROUGH!
I'M SORRY.
I DON'T SEE ANY PRINCE CONCERT ON THE LIST, SIR.
BUT THAT'S IMPOS--
THERE!
I WASN'T EVEN SURE PRINCE WOULD ACTUALLY BE THERE, BUT...
JOHNNY HA
"MADHOUSE"! I BET THAT'S IT! HOW MUCH FOR ONE TICKET, PLEASE?
HMM
160 FRANCS.
HOW MUCH?!
THAT'S MORE THAN BERCY!
MADHOUSE
MICHEL SARDOU
...HE HAD DONE THE SAME THING LAST YEAR, AT THE SAME VENUE, THE "NEW," SO...
...I BOUGHT A TICKET.

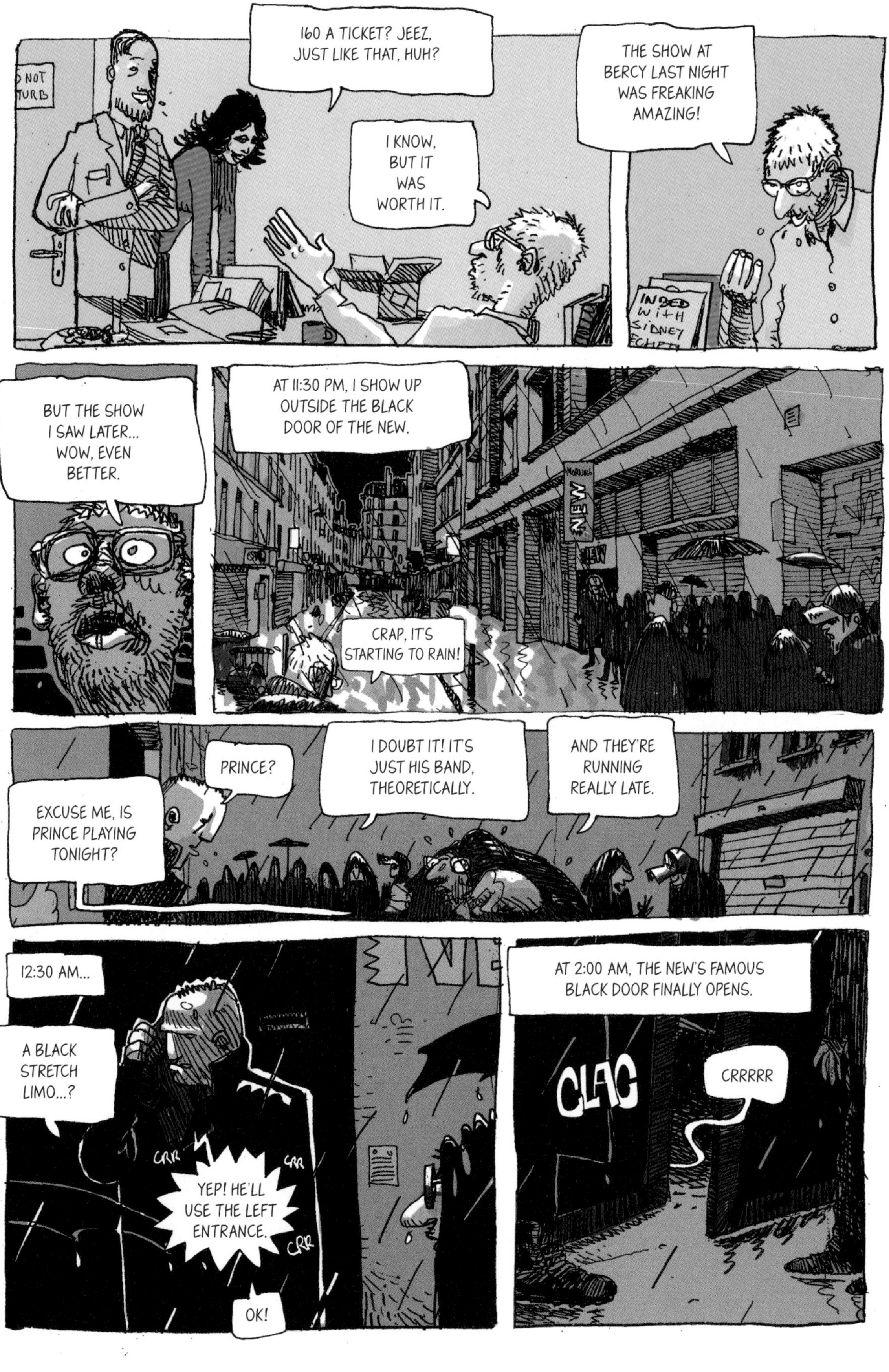
D NOT
TURB
160 A TICKET? JEEZ, JUST LIKE THAT, HUH?
I KNOW, BUT IT WAS WORTH IT.
THE SHOW AT BERCY LAST NIGHT WAS FREAKING AMAZING!
BUT THE SHOW I SAW LATER... WOW, EVEN BETTER.
AT 11:30 PM, I SHOW UP OUTSIDE THE BLACK DOOR OF THE NEW.
NEW
CRAP, IT'S STARTING TO RAIN!
EXCUSE ME, IS PRINCE PLAYING TONIGHT?
PRINCE?
I DOUBT IT! IT'S JUST HIS BAND, THEORETICALLY.
AND THEY'RE RUNNING REALLY LATE.
12:30 AM...
A BLACK STRETCH LIMO...?
CRR
CRR
YEP! HE'LL USE THE LEFT ENTRANCE.
CRR
OK!
AT 2:00 AM, THE NEW'S FAMOUS BLACK DOOR FINALLY OPENS.
CLAC
CRRRRR

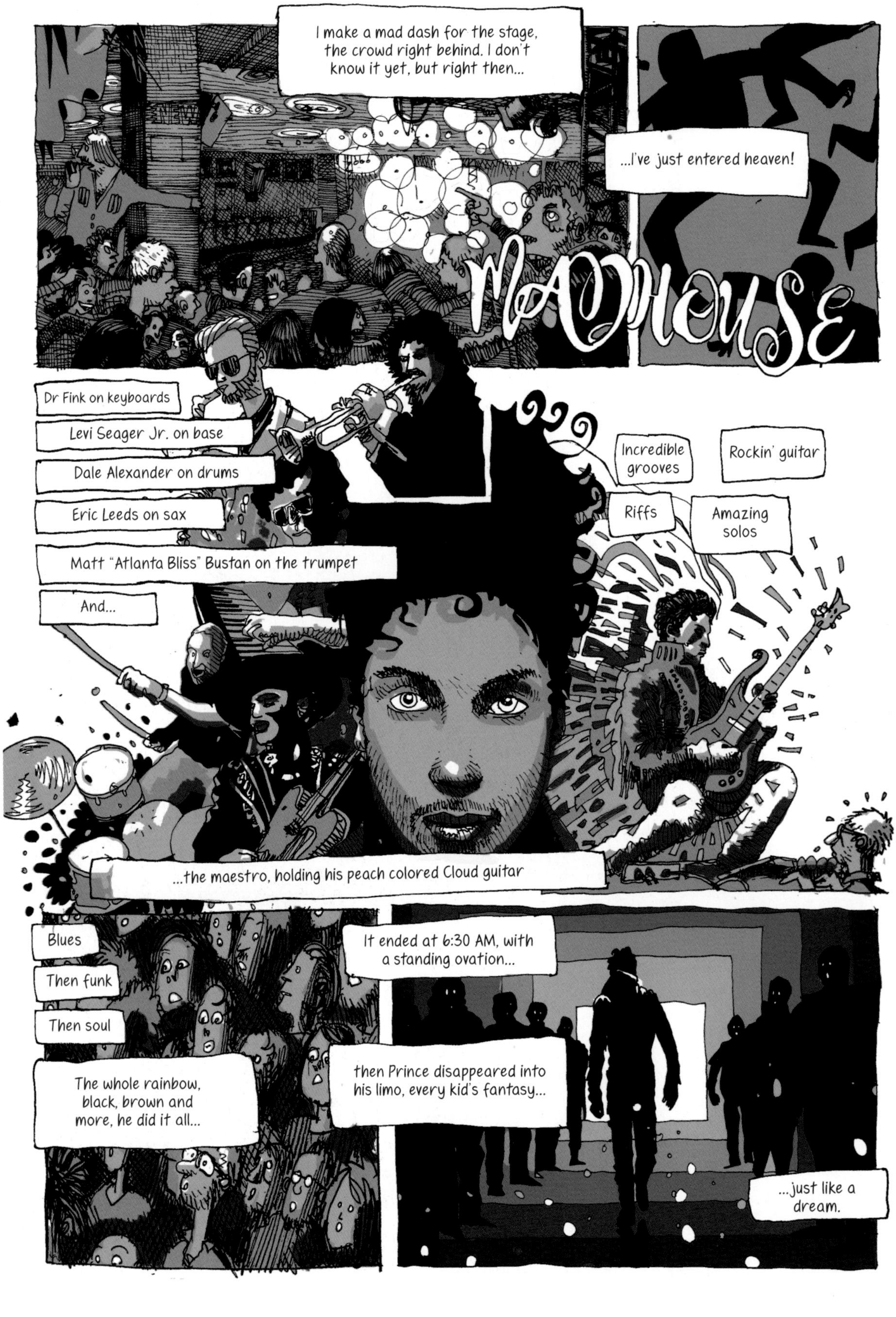

I make a mad dash for the stage, the crowd right behind. I don't know it yet, but right then...
...I've just entered heaven!
MADHOUSE
Dr Fink on keyboards
Levi Seager Jr. on base
Dale Alexander on drums
Eric Leeds on sax
Matt "Atlanta Bliss" Bustan on the trumpet
And...
Incredible grooves
Rockin' guitar
Riffs
Amazing solos
...the maestro, holding his peach colored Cloud guitar
Blues
Then funk
Then soul
The whole rainbow, black, brown and more, he did it all...
It ended at 6:30 AM, with a standing ovation...
then Prince disappeared into his limo, every kid's fantasy...
...just like a dream.

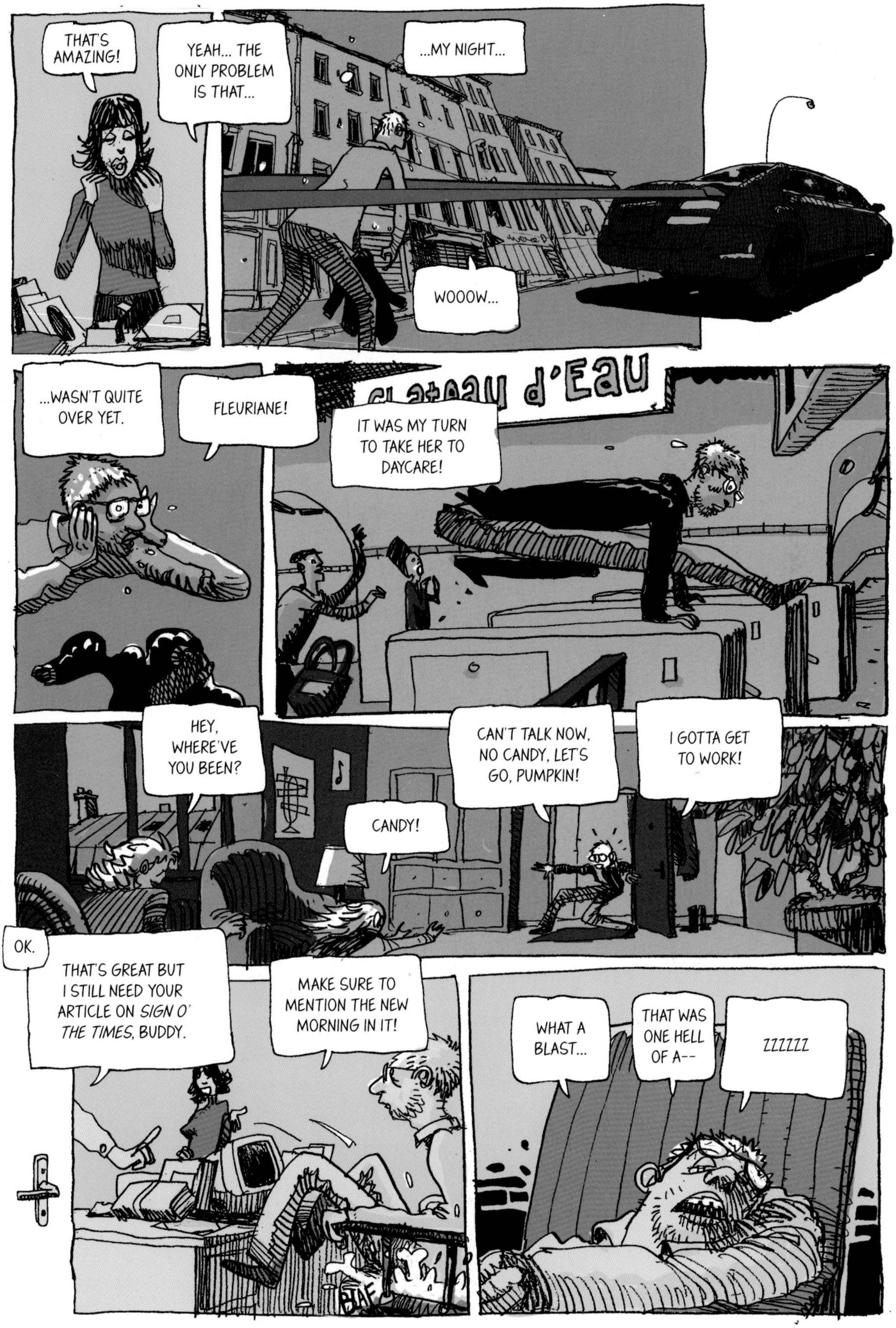

THAT'S AMAZING!
YEAH... THE ONLY PROBLEM IS THAT...
...MY NIGHT...
WOOOW...
...WASN'T QUITE OVER YET.
FLEURIANE!
IT WAS MY TURN TO TAKE HER TO DAYCARE!
HEY, WHERE'VE YOU BEEN?
CANDY!
CAN'T TALK NOW, NO CANDY, LET'S GO, PUMPKIN!
I GOTTA GET TO WORK!
OK.
THAT'S GREAT BUT I STILL NEED YOUR ARTICLE ON *SIGN O' THE TIMES*, BUDDY.
MAKE SURE TO MENTION THE NEW MORNING IN IT!
WHAT A BLAST...
THAT WAS ONE HELL OF A--
ZZZZZZ

In 1984, *Purple Rain* had sealed Prince's membership in the very selective club of superstars with global audiences. Three years later, a legendary double album, *Sign O' the Times*, would prove to everyone, skeptics included, that the artist not only appealed to the masses, but that he was also a musician of exceptional range.

The two albums that followed *Purple Rain, Around the World in a Day* in 1985 and then *Parade* in 1986, had already distinguished themselves by a remarkable quality of inspiration and production. The sumptuous *Parade*, in particular, had impressed listeners by its diversity and its musical richness. Twelve irrefutable tracts on the album, including the hit single *Kiss* and the irresistible *Sometimes It Snows in April*, the most melancholic ballad in the world. But a year later, *Sign O' the Times* managed to set the bar even higher, with its density, diversity, the quality of the lyrics and the melodic richness. In the eyes of the critics as well as a large percentage of the mainstream audience, it was an artistic pinnacle in a career that had already seen many; it was Prince's masterpiece – and for once, the qualifier was not an exaggeration.

Almost all the genres and styles that the artist had used over the course of his decade-long career – funk, soul, jazz, rock, pop, electronics – were brought together here for musical fireworks of rare intensity, filled with contrasts and sudden breaks in rhythm. A total musical creation in which each component was a jewel. An absolute artistic triumph. The purists claimed Prince would never do better than that album...

Sign O' the Times movie poster. Hastily cobbled together from the last three European concerts on the tour, it did not meet with the success Prince had anticipated.

The album would sell more than four million copies over time. A more than respectable figure, of course, in a musical landscape where the offer was overabundant. But for Prince, it was almost a disappointment. Especially since, for probably the first time, this unquestionable discographic achievement did not result in commercial success in the U.S. In fact, only Europe had truly celebrated *Sign O' the Times* as the expression of princely genius that it was, namely through massive purchases of the album.

> THE ALBUM THAT WAS RELEASED IN 1987 PROMISED TO BE A KEY MOMENT IN PRINCE'S CAREER. IN REALITY, IT WOULD BE EVEN BETTER: *SIGN O' THE TIMES* SPREAD ITS SPLENDOROUS SOUNDSCAPE ACROSS A DOUBLE ALBUM THAT DAZZLED LISTENERS FROM THE FIRST TRACK TO THE LAST. PRINCE'S CATHEDRAL.

This explains why the tour organized as soon as the album was released was, in the end, almost exclusively European. A shortened tour, actually. Aware of the more than mixed commercial reception reserved by the American public for his double album, magnificent though it was, Prince abruptly decided to cancel the fall 1987 dates in the United States. At the same time, also deviating from the original plan, he arranged for the filming of a live recording of his last three European concerts in order to provide the material for his next feature film. This would become *Sign O' the Times*, which hit U.S. movie theaters at the end of November. The film suffered from limited distribution and a lack of organization, and only attracted a moderate number of moviegoers. Subsequent video sales, on the other hand, would prove more satisfying over time. Dazzling on an artistic level, the *Sign O' the Times* adventure had the added benefit of strengthening the ties between Prince and his European audiences. The man who had never set foot in Europe until the 1980s understood that there were fans there to cater to, fans who were probably quite different from his American ones.

France, in that regard, quickly grew to hold a special place in the musician's heart. **The artist loved Paris, which was only too happy to return the favor, and the French capital would serve as the setting for several after-shows that have remained memorable in the princely annals, in particular at the New Morning, a Parisian jazz club whose Prince connection remains a claim to fame to this day.**

The entrance to the New Morning jazz club in Paris, in the 10th arrondissement. Over time, Prince became a regular there.

1988
LOVESEXY

PRINCE AND THE MOVIES: *BATMAN*

Why the collaborations? It's probably partly because he needs to bounce back commercially after the lackluster performance of his *Lovesexy* album that Prince becomes interested in Batman, Tim Burton's new film project— and probably also because he happens to be a longtime fan of the Gotham vigilante. Bingo: he is so enthralled by the little he sees of the film that he makes an entire album for it, which will give his career a major boost.

London, December 1988.

PERSONALLY, I'M A FAN. SO TRUST AN OLD PRO.

PRINCE IS *THE* MUSICIAN WE NEED FOR THIS SOUNDTRACK.

I JUST ATTENDED TWO OF HIS CONCERTS HERE IN LONDON, AND FRANKLY, I'VE NEVER SEEN ANYTHING THAT POWERFUL, BUT...

...I DON'T KNOW IF HIS MUSIC IS A GOOD FIT FOR MY VISION OF THE FILM.

QUIT THINKING SO MUCH, WILL YA?

YOU WOULDN'T WANT TO DISAPPOINT UNCLE JACK NOW, WOULD YA?

A few days later...

THIS TIM BURTON GUY SEEMS VERY TALENTED AND HE WANTS YOU TO WORK ON HIS *BATMAN* PROJECT.

HE SAYS HE PUT TWO OF YOUR SONGS IN A WORKING COPY OF THE FILM: *1999* AND *BABY I'M A STAR*.

...AND THAT WITH YOUR PERMISSION, HE'D LIKE TO INCLUDE OTHER SONGS.

UNLESS YOU'D BE OPEN TO WRITING SOME NEW ONES.

HMM... THIS ISN'T THE BEST TIME FOR ME. *LOVESEXY* FAILED TO PERFORM AS I HAD HOPED AND I'M ALREADY THINKING ABOUT MORE ALBUMS.

BEFORE HE HUNG UP, HE SAID HE WAS SHOOTING IN LONDON AT THE MOMENT AND HE INVITED YOU TO THE SET TO DISCUSS ALL THIS.

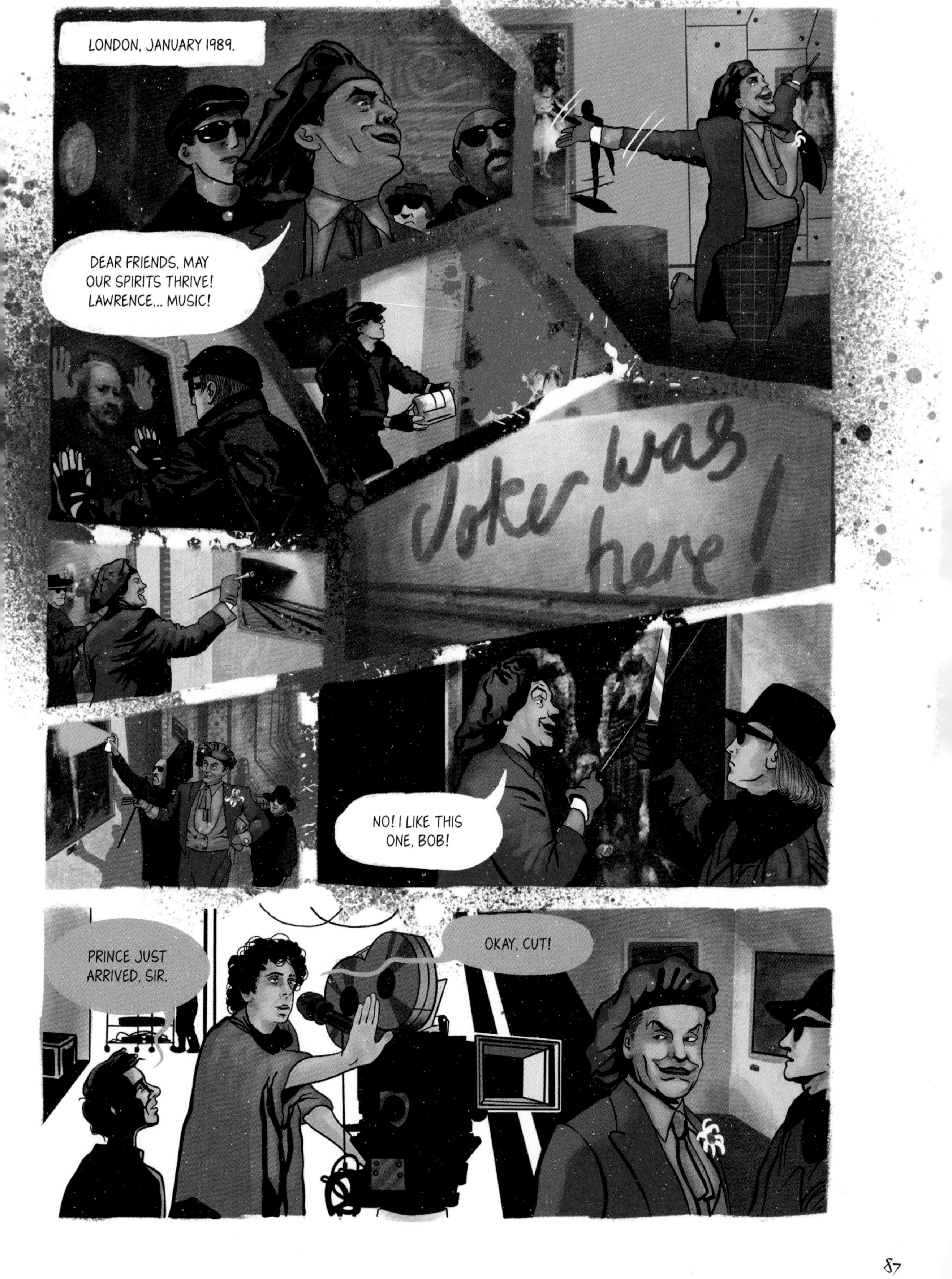
LONDON, JANUARY 1989.
DEAR FRIENDS, MAY OUR SPIRITS THRIVE! LAWRENCE... MUSIC!
Joker was here!
NO! I LIKE THIS ONE, BOB!
PRINCE JUST ARRIVED, SIR.
OKAY, CUT!

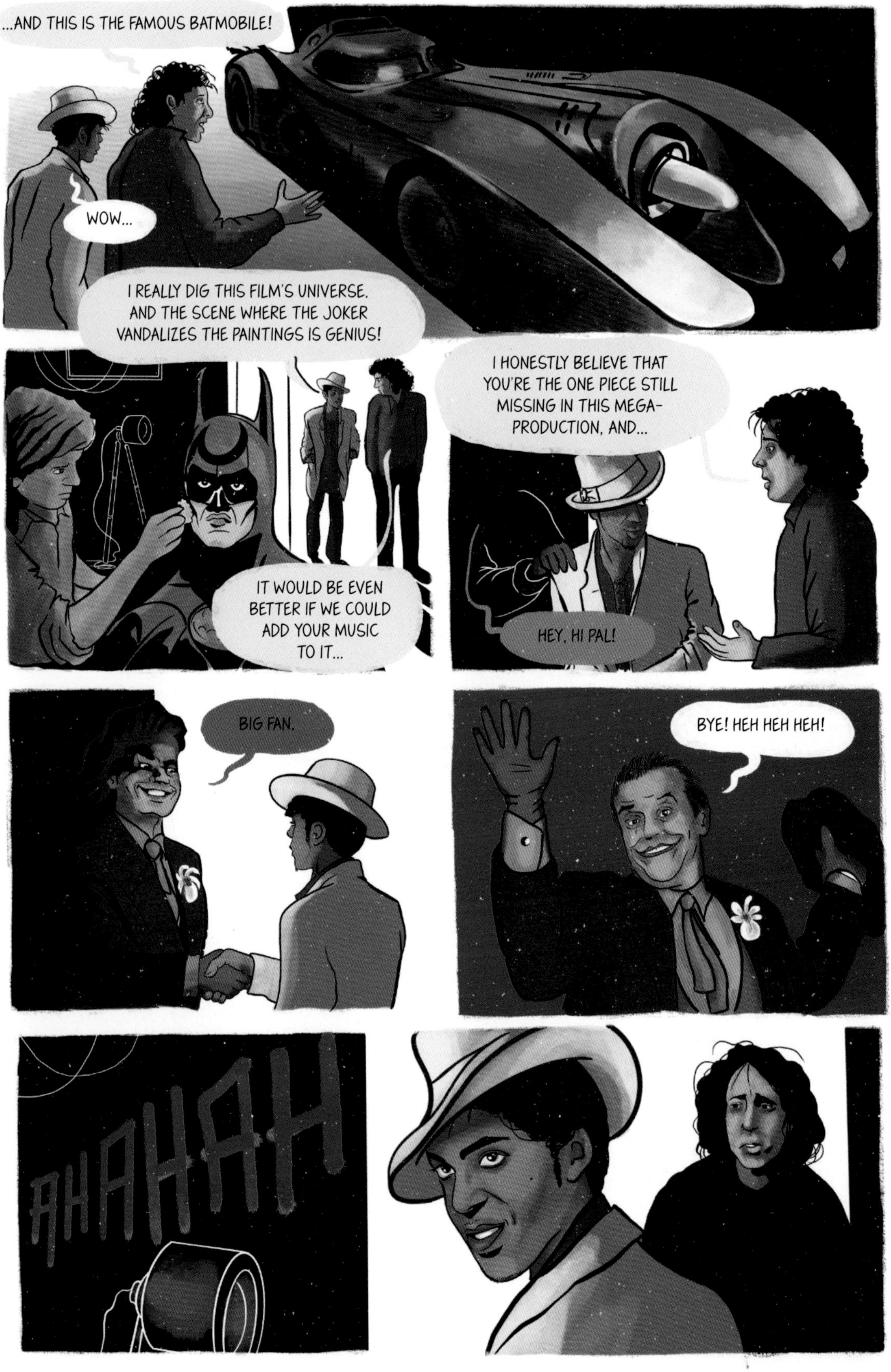
...AND THIS IS THE FAMOUS BATMOBILE!
WOW...
I REALLY DIG THIS FILM'S UNIVERSE. AND THE SCENE WHERE THE JOKER VANDALIZES THE PAINTINGS IS GENIUS!
IT WOULD BE EVEN BETTER IF WE COULD ADD YOUR MUSIC TO IT...
I HONESTLY BELIEVE THAT YOU'RE THE ONE PIECE STILL MISSING IN THIS MEGA-PRODUCTION, AND...
HEY, HI PAL!
BIG FAN.
BYE! HEH HEH HEH!
AHAHAH

Excited about the project, Prince wanted to get to the studio at once to start....

...but he knew that first, he had to finish the Japanese part of his Lovesexy Tour.

UNTIL WHEN?

FEBRUARY 15TH, BOSS.

Back in Paisley Park, it's a rigorous schedule of Batman sessions.

After just a few weeks, Prince hands over 11 tracks to the producers. Many more than necessary...

They decide to release an album "inspired by the film," whereas the real soundtrack, composed by Danny Elfman, comes out as a separate album.

The outcome for Prince?

A huge hit.

T hirty years later, we tend to forget that *Batman* has not always been part of our cinematic landscape, and that there was a time when the vigilante of Gotham embodied a real novelty on big screens around the world. The late 1980s, for example. At that time, the character was still just an icon from the world of comics and TV. It would take the joint participation, at the instigation of Warner Bros Studios, of several Hollywood heavyweights – director Tim Burton and actors Jack Nicholson, Kim Basinger and Michael Keaton (and incidentally the blessing of Bob Kane, the co-creator of the Batman comic book series) before the Batman could really consider entering the pantheon of mythical heroes.

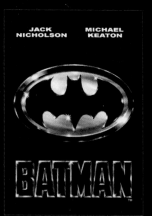

That's when Prince joined this group project. Unlike Burton who was not particularly a fan of the character, the musician was

Jack Nicholson as The Joker. His spectacular performance vastly contributed to the international success of Tim Burton's film.

a long-time admirer of Batman's exploits in the comic books. So he enthusiastically agreed to the idea of working on the film, since Burton and Nicholson (the actor was closely involved with the production of the film) had pre-selected two of his songs (*1999* and *Baby I'm a Star*) to include on the soundtrack. What they had actually planned was a double soundtrack: on the one hand a classic instrumental original score by composer Danny Elfman, which would ultimately be sold separately, under the title *Batman: Original Motion Picture Score*; and on the other hand a selection of hits taken from the charts of the time, to use as thematic character signatures. The kind of collaboration they envisioned for Prince would change drastically when he visited the film set in London in January 1989. Fascinated by what he saw there, and now more convinced than ever of his need to be a part of this project, an enraptured Prince decided to

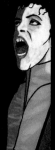

ONCE AGAIN, THE WORLD OF MOVIEMAKING WAS TO APPEAR ON THE PRINCELY HORIZON. TIM BURTON'S *BATMAN* WAS A GLOBAL PHENOMENON AND A BOX OFFICE HIT. PRINCE'S SOUNDTRACK FOR THE MOVIE WAS ALSO A TRIUMPH.

titled *Batman: Motion Picture Soundtrack*. A complete nine-track album produced in just six weeks, between mid-February and the end of March 1989. Fast enough to be released in June, shortly before the release of Burton's actual film, and thus perfect for cross promotion as a loss leader.

It was a good call. *Batman*, the movie, was an international hit that performed beautifully at the box office (over 400 million dollars for an initial budget of 35 million, which, at the time, made it one of the five most profitable films of all time), which of course helped provide equal visibility to the other works of creative expression and the merchandising that came out alongside the film.

As for Prince's album, it sold four and a half million copies. Not too shabby. The boss hadn't lost his touch.

put aside all his ongoing projects upon returning to Paisley Park and to focus on his contribution to *Batman*. This would take the form of a counter-offer he submitted to Burton and Nicholson: not to use pre-existing songs, but songs that Prince would create especially for the film. They signed off on it and he got to work right away--especially seeing as this decision was probably not without ulterior motives. The (relative) failure of the 1988 *Lovesexy*, the album that followed *Sign O' the Times*, was forcing Prince to find a way to reinvent himself--and toward that end, doing the soundtrack for the new Tim Burton probably wouldn't be the worst option in the world. That, then, is how a purely Prince album came about,

1989
BATMAN

1991

DIAMONDS AND PEARLS...

What a journey! Only a dozen years after his first timid steps in the big leagues, Prince is at the very top of the game. A planetary superstar, he is also at the height of his creativity. He can do whatever he wants and can get whatever he wants. And his new, super talented band New Power Generation seems to perfectly summarize his expectations. Two dazzling albms, *Diamonds and Pearls* and *Love Symbol*, materialize this moment of grace.

ART: Christelle Pécout

THE NEW POWER GENERATION. THIS IS THE BAND THAT CAME AFTER THE LOVESEXY BAND.

"WELCOME TO THE NEW POWER GENERATION": THE SENTENCE ACTUALLY APPEARS IN THE INTRO TO "EYE NO" ON THE *LOVESEXY* ALBUM.

A PHRASE FANS CHANT LIKE A SLOGAN AT HIS CONCERTS.

NEW POWER GENERATION

NEW POWER GENERATION WAS ALSO A TRACK ON *GRAFFITI BRIDGE*, WHICH CAME OUT IN 1990...

...AND EVEN THE NAME OF A BROADCAST DEDICATED TO PRINCE THAT AIRED IN DECEMBER 1990 ON KMOJ, A LOCAL MINNEAPOLIS RADIO STATION.

KMOJ 89.9 Radio

IT THEREFORE MADE SENSE WHEN, IN 1991, THE STAR'S NEW ALBUM, **DIAMONDS AND PEARLS**, WAS PRESENTED AS...

PRINCE & THE NEW POWER GENERATION

BUT WHO BETTER THAN THE FOUNDING MEMBERS TO TALK ABOUT THE...

NPG

NEW POWER GENERATION

THE BUNKERS. THAT'S WHERE I FIRST MET PRINCE IN LATE 1988.

MICHAEL BLAND

WE JAMMED THERE BEFORE PURSUING EACH OTHER FOR A FEW MONTHS: INVITATIONS TO AFTERPARTIES, PRIVATE LISTENING OF THE *BATMAN* SOUNDTRACK, ETC.

AND IT WAS DURING A PARTY AT PAISLEY PARK FOR BON JOVI THAT HE OFFERED ME THE JOB.

PRINCE WANTED TO CREATE A BIG BAND WITH A PRIMARILY BLACK FEEL TO IT.

IN THE FIRST ITERATION OF THE NEW POWER GENERATION, WE EVEN HAD A TRIO OF DANCERS / RAPPERS, THE GAME BOYZ.

THEN AGAIN, BACK THEN, HIP-HOP WAS ALL OVER THE SMALL SCREEN, LIKE VH1 AND MTV. AND HE WANTED TO REJUVENATE HIS MUSIC BY FOLLOWING THE TRENDS.

SONNY THOMPSON, AKA SONNY T.

THE LEGENDARY DR. FINK WAS ON HIS WAY OUT AND I WAS GIVEN THE DAUNTING TASK OF REPLACING HIM IN 1991 DURING A CONCERT AT THE GLAM SLAM.

I'VE BEEN WITH THEM EVER SINCE.

TOMMY "BARBARELLA" ELM

ME, I SPLIT AFTER THE DIAMONDS AND PEARLS TOUR IN THE SUMMER OF '92.

ROSIE GAINES

TOO MUCH TESTOSTERONE FOR MY TASTE... MORRIS HAYES REPLACED ME.

HI, EVERYBODY!

MORRIS HAYES

AT THE END OF '93, I LEFT THE BAND TOO, TO BECOME PRESIDENT OF PAISLEY PARK RECORDS.

LEVI SEACER, JR.

BAD MOVE: THE LABEL SHUT DOWN FEBRUARY IST, 1994. AND LATER, I GOT INTO A DISPUTE WITH THE BOSS OVER ROYALTIES...

BUMMER. WE WERE ALL GREAT FRIENDS.

THE BOSS WAS MOSTLY MAD AT WARNER. THEIR VISION OF THE BIZ WAS STARTING TO SERIOUSLY DIFFER FROM HIS.

SONNY THOMPSON, AKA SONNY T

REMINDS ME OF THE STUNT HE PULLED ON THEM WITH *GET OFF.*

IN MAY OF '91, WE WERE RECORDING THE SONG. PRINCE LOVED IT AND WANTED TO RELEASE THE SINGLE RIGHT AWAY...

...WITHOUT WAITING FOR WARNER'S INPUT.

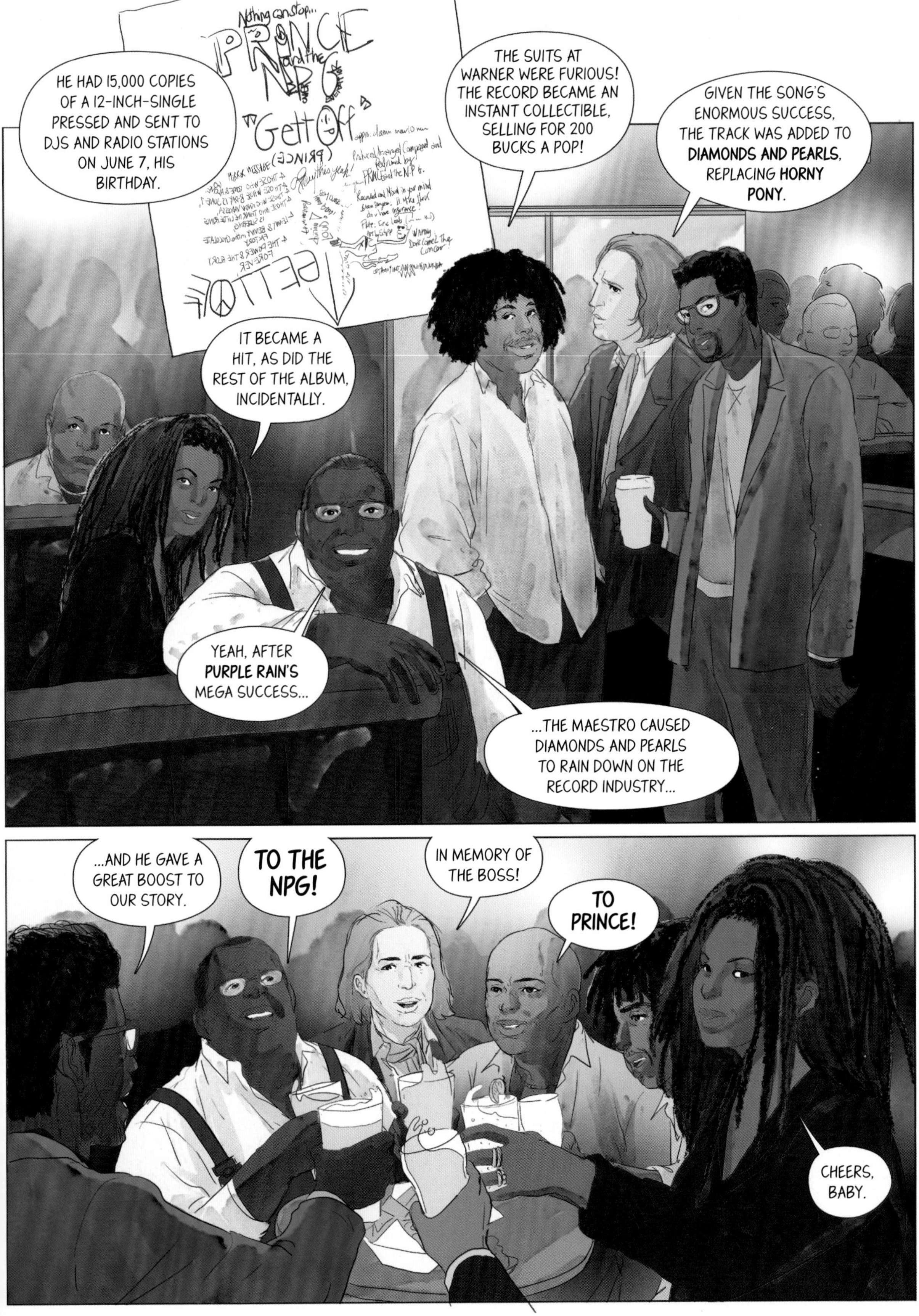
HE HAD 15,000 COPIES OF A 12-INCH-SINGLE PRESSED AND SENT TO DJS AND RADIO STATIONS ON JUNE 7, HIS BIRTHDAY.
Nothing can stop... PRINCE and the NPG
"Gett Off"
THE SUITS AT WARNER WERE FURIOUS! THE RECORD BECAME AN INSTANT COLLECTIBLE, SELLING FOR 200 BUCKS A POP!
GIVEN THE SONG'S ENORMOUS SUCCESS, THE TRACK WAS ADDED TO **DIAMONDS AND PEARLS**, REPLACING **HORNY PONY**.
IT BECAME A HIT, AS DID THE REST OF THE ALBUM, INCIDENTALLY.
YEAH, AFTER **PURPLE RAIN'S** MEGA SUCCESS...
...THE MAESTRO CAUSED DIAMONDS AND PEARLS TO RAIN DOWN ON THE RECORD INDUSTRY...
...AND HE GAVE A GREAT BOOST TO OUR STORY.
TO THE NPG!
IN MEMORY OF THE BOSS!
TO PRINCE!
CHEERS, BABY.

From the album *1999* to the album *Love Symbol*, this was Prince's Golden Decade. David Bowie, Pink Floyd, the Beatles and so many others: most major artists and bands experience a great decade, where everything they undertake turns to gold, artistically speaking. But it is rare, on the other hand, for such genius to last beyond ten years... And Prince would follow in that tradition. At the start of the 1990s, the Kid, back in the saddle thanks to the commercial success of the *Batman* film soundtrack, was bursting with ideas and desires--starting with the desire to surround himself with a new artistic team. His band The Revolution, which had brilliantly accompanied his entry into the 1980s, had long since disbanded. On the other hand, many newcomers had entered the artist's inner circle, such as drummer Michael Bland, keyboardist Tommy Barbarella, dancer Tony Mosley, bassist Sonny Thompson and backing vocalist Mayte Garcia.

That would be the backbone of the band The New Power Generation - quickly transformed into NPG by the fans –, which,

in fluctuating formations of up to seventeen musicians and dancers (!), would perform alongside Prince for around ten years, until the early 2000s. The name of the band had in fact actually first appeared in the form of a song, as one of the tracks on the *Lovesexy* album in 1988, then two years later in the credits of the film *Graffiti Bridge* – the only true flop in this otherwise exceptionally fruitful period. With The New Power Generation, a formation with impressive rhythmic power, both big and subtle, the musician would cause sparks to fly, especially with the new album he had been preparing for months, a few nuggets of which he had unveiled in advance, such as the intriguing *Gett Off* which he performed at the MTV Awards in early September 1991 using sexually charged staging. *Diamonds and Pearls*, that's the title of the album, came out on October 1st, 1991 and won over everyone right off the bat - critics and the mainstream audience alike.

With thirteen great tracks including a few obvious hits (the addictive *Cream* and

Prince on MTV. He was one of the icons of American music heavily showcased by the music video channel.

Prince in 1990. A rare image, which, as a counterpoint to the usual, sexually charged photos of the artist at that time, gives him a surprisingly youthful air.

the seminal *Gett Off*, both enhanced by particularly polished big-budget music videos), all of them impeccably produced, the album was an immediate hit. It would go on to sell some six million copies – apparently, the people who thought that the Kid was artistically finished after *Graffiti Bridge* were wrong. The tour that followed was of the same ilk: triumphant. In short, Prince's newest creation was a masterstroke.

However (there's always a however), there still remained the pebble in his shoe known as the record company. The relationship between Prince and Warner had been notoriously difficult ever since their first meeting and the contract that bound them, and it fluctuated depending on the period, going from tense to outright antagonistic. Prince could not understand why his record company didn't automatically support him with enthusiasm (and with the necessary means) on all his projects.

As for Warner, they failed to contain or even channel the creativity of their protégé: he was too excessive, too erratic – and he almost never went with the direction they wanted, such as, for example, with the *Best Of* project he was insistently urged to do and which he rejected with similar energy. Inevitably, both sides would get upset. But the people at Warner, who were above all else music industry businessmen, knew their way around money. Rather than letting their artist go to a different label, which Prince had hinted at more and more openly, they tried to win him over by offering him a position as vice-president and a lucrative contract for his next ten albums. The arrangement would, temporarily, ease the tensions between them. But in the end, the misunderstanding only got worse and turned into an outright crisis. **By the end of 1992, when the *Love Symbol* album, a new album by Prince and the New Power Generation (and the last major exploit of the artistically blessed decade that the artist had just gone through), was released, war had been declared for good.**

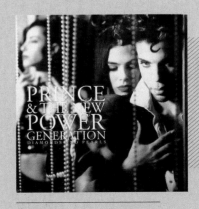

1991
DIAMONDS ANS PEARLS

1992 - 1997

TOUGH TIMES...

At this point in his career, Prince's adversarial relationship with his record company had deteriorated to such an extent that there was no going back. Despite his efforts to do everything to honor the current contract, the records that come out are little or badly promoted, which affects sales. Bad vibes all around. At the end of 1996, the premature death of his newborn son helps make this period one of the darkest in the artist's career.

ART: Barrack Rima

Winter 2016.

AT 16, I WAS ALREADY A PROFESSIONAL DANCER. WHEN MY MOM SAW PRINCE IN CONCERT IN BARCELONA ON JULY 25, 1990, SHE DECIDED I SHOULD DANCE FOR HIM, AND SHE LOOKED FOR A WAY TO GET HIM TO NOTICE ME. WE WERE LIVING IN FRANKFURT AT THE TIME, AND...

...during a show in Manheim, she managed to get a video of me to Kirk Johnson, one of the Game Boyz.

And just a few minutes later...

HEY! PRINCE SAW YOUR TAPE, HE WANTS TO MEET YOU.

...I found myself backstage at the Nude Tour in front of my idol. Hypnotized.

H-HI... I'M... I'M MAYTE GARCIA.

I didn't even notice that he was falling in love with me.

And indeed, our destiny together was sealed that night of August 8, 1990.

For better...

...AND FOR WORSE...

My 18th birthday marked the beginning of my collaboration with Prince and the NPG.

I moved to Minneapolis and, after a few months, I became the main dancer, replacing Diamond, Pearl and the Game Boyz.

I had become his muse...

Up until...

HEY, GUESS WHERE I AM, BABY!

BARCELONA! WHERE YOU FIRST SAW ME IN CONCERT! IT'S THE PERFECT MOMENT TO ASK YOU THE BIG QUESTION, SWEETHEART...

We were married on February 14, 1996, Valentine's Day.

To him, I was "the most beautiful girl in the world..."

WHERE ARE YOU TAKING ME?

TO HONOLULU!

Shortly thereafter, we were expecting a child.

We were truly living a fairytale.

That year, just like Michael Jackson and Madonna, he had signed a lucrative contract with his label...

...without realizing that he was also signing away his artistic freedom.

CARMEN ELECTRA WAS ALREADY BAD ENOUGH, BUT GOLD NIGGA IS MUCH WORSE!

Criticism, mismanagement, constraints and commercial one-upmanship... a boss-employee relationship that Prince tried to avoid like the plague.

HE'S RELEASING ALBUMS LIKE A MACHINE. THAT LITTLE DIVA NEEDS TO CALM DOWN!

As the war raged openly, and since Warner owned the rights to the name "Prince," he took on a new identity.

This was a chance for him to separate from his past as well as reach a new spiritual level, which involved changing one's name.

Our baby boy was born on October 16, 1996...

...and he died six days later.

While promoting Emancipation on The Oprah Winfrey Show, the question came up...

WHAT IS THE STATUS OF YOUR BABY?

OPRAH

Self-preservation? Denial? I don't know. Be that as it may, Prince lied that day...

OUR FAMILY EXISTS.

...And I didn't say anything... Out of love for him.

WE'RE JUST BEGINNING IT, AND WE GOT MANY KIDS TO HAVE AND A LONG WAY TO GO.

WORKING WAS THE ONLY WAY FOR HIM TO COPE WITH THAT TRAGEDY. HE WENT ON TOUR AND HE PLAYED HIS MUSIC.

TO THE POINT OF EXHAUSTION.

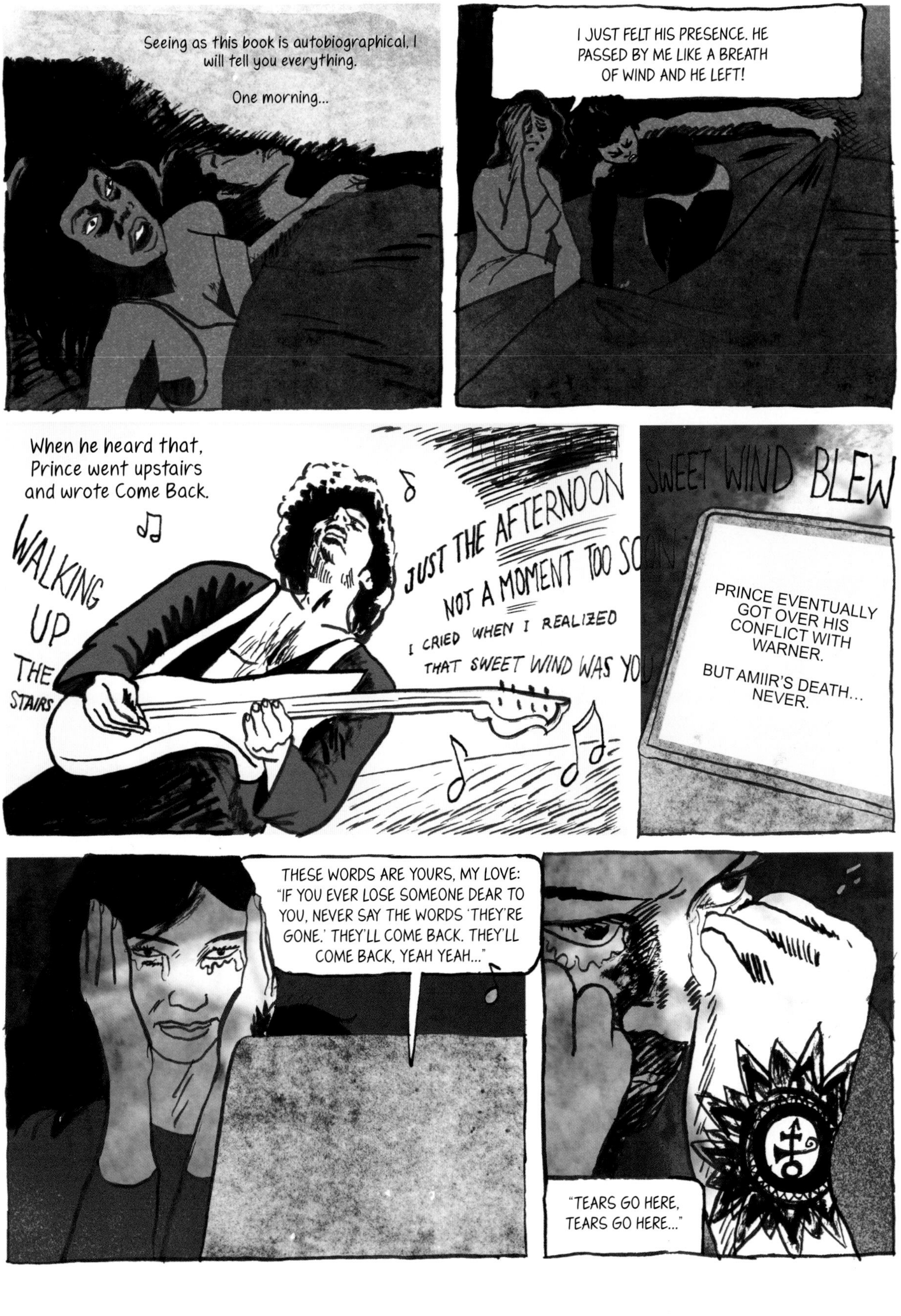
Seeing as this book is autobiographical, I will tell you everything.
One morning...
I JUST FELT HIS PRESENCE. HE PASSED BY ME LIKE A BREATH OF WIND AND HE LEFT!
When he heard that, Prince went upstairs and wrote Come Back.
WALKING UP THE STAIRS
JUST THE AFTERNOON
NOT A MOMENT TOO SOON
I CRIED WHEN I REALIZED
THAT SWEET WIND WAS YOU
SWEET WIND BLEW
PRINCE EVENTUALLY GOT OVER HIS CONFLICT WITH WARNER.
BUT AMIIR'S DEATH... NEVER.
THESE WORDS ARE YOURS, MY LOVE: "IF YOU EVER LOSE SOMEONE DEAR TO YOU, NEVER SAY THE WORDS 'THEY'RE GONE.' THEY'LL COME BACK. THEY'LL COME BACK, YEAH YEAH..."
"TEARS GO HERE, TEARS GO HERE..."

By the mid-1990s, as his fortieth loomed on the horizon (already!), Prince was headed for stormy weather. He had succeeded in virtually everything he had done up until then, including the very successful *Love Symbol* album in 1992, which sold three million copies. But the recurring conflict with Warner, his record label, would precipitate the crisis once and for all. In 1993, Warner management decided to start using a more forceful approach and imposed on Prince the compilation album that he had stubbornly rejected for years: *The Hits / The B Sides*, which became the title, a hefty 56-title anthology of Prince songs, was not an unworthy proposal; it was just the opposite, in fact, and it even helped fans rediscover titles they might have had forgotten. But the fact that this commercial stunt was implemented against the artist's explicit wishes triggered a sequence of open hostilities.

Prince announced that from then on, he would stop using his name, choosing instead to call himself the ideogram, a synthesis of the male and female symbols, which he had used as the cover art for the *Love Symbol* album. The word was unpronounceable, of course, which immediately turned into a puzzle for the media: if he no longer wanted to be called Prince, what were people supposed to call him? This would be known as the TAFKAP chapter - not the most glorious one in the Kid's career. Forced to find a way to designate the artist they were talking about, the media (especially in the U.S.) coined an acronym: "The Artist Formerly Known As Prince," a half-baked formula, which, for lack of a better option, would be used to designate Prince for several years, both in the written press and on television and radio stations.

Meanwhile, he continued to release records albums on the Warner Bros label: *The Black Album*, and another compilation, *1-800-NEW-FUNK*, in 1994, both of which were badly promoted and therefore performed poorly. That same year, an album of ten unreleased tracks

> **STORMY WEATHER WAS ON THE HORIZON... AS THE CONFLICT WITH HIS RECORD LABEL GOT WORSE, PRINCE HAD TO GO THROUGH THE MOST PAINFUL ORDEAL A HUMAN BEING CAN ENDURE: THE LOSS OF A CHILD.**

Prince at the time when he performed live on French TV, his cheek adorned with a message that was... illegible.

was released as well, *Come*, which failed to do much better. That marked the beginning of an increasingly confused and chaotic period, where some of his albums continued to appear on the Warner label, so as to honor the contract then still in effect (this was notably the case with the albums *The Gold Experience* in 1995, *Chaos and Disorder* in 1996 and *The Vault: Old Friends 4 Sale* in 1999), while other projects such as *Exodus* (1995) were released directly on the artist's label, *NPG Records*, and distributed by various companies (Arista, Columbia, Universal, EMI, etc). It was also during this period that Prince, still contractually bound to Warner regardless of his claims to the opposite, appeared in public with the word "slave" written in big letters on his cheek, to symbolically express his self-perceived status as the subject of forced submission. The year 1996, however, appeared to be off to a much better start. Prince was preparing his first post-Warner album, *Emancipation* (the album's booklet opened with a photo of the Kid taken from the side, showing the famous "slave" mention on the cheek), which would be released on his own label, NPG Records, and distributed by EMI. It was a substantial work: no less than a triple album with a sixty-minute running time per album, each done in a very specific musical register. With the exception of a few covers of songs by other artists, all the songs were new.

And then, on the flip side of this hectic period, the personal side, there was a ray of sunshine: from Prince's ongoing relationship with the dancer Mayte Garcia, who had been with the NPG team for several years already, a child would be born. The two were married in February and little Amiir was due to come into the world in October.. **Alas, the baby was born with a rare malformation of the cranium. He underwent surgery, but died six days after his birth.**

1992
LOVE SYMBOL

1996
CHAOS AND DISORDER

1996
EMANCIPATION

1998 - 2000

...AND REBIRTH

How do you recover from a personal tragedy? For Prince, salvation will come through art and creation. He loses himself in his work for a long period of time and the result is impressive: a gigantic American tour that people still remember, the Jam of the Year Tour, and, above all, the release of one album after another in rapid succession in 1998 and 1999. Not to mention gambling on the new medium everyone is talking about: the internet.

ART: Toru Terada

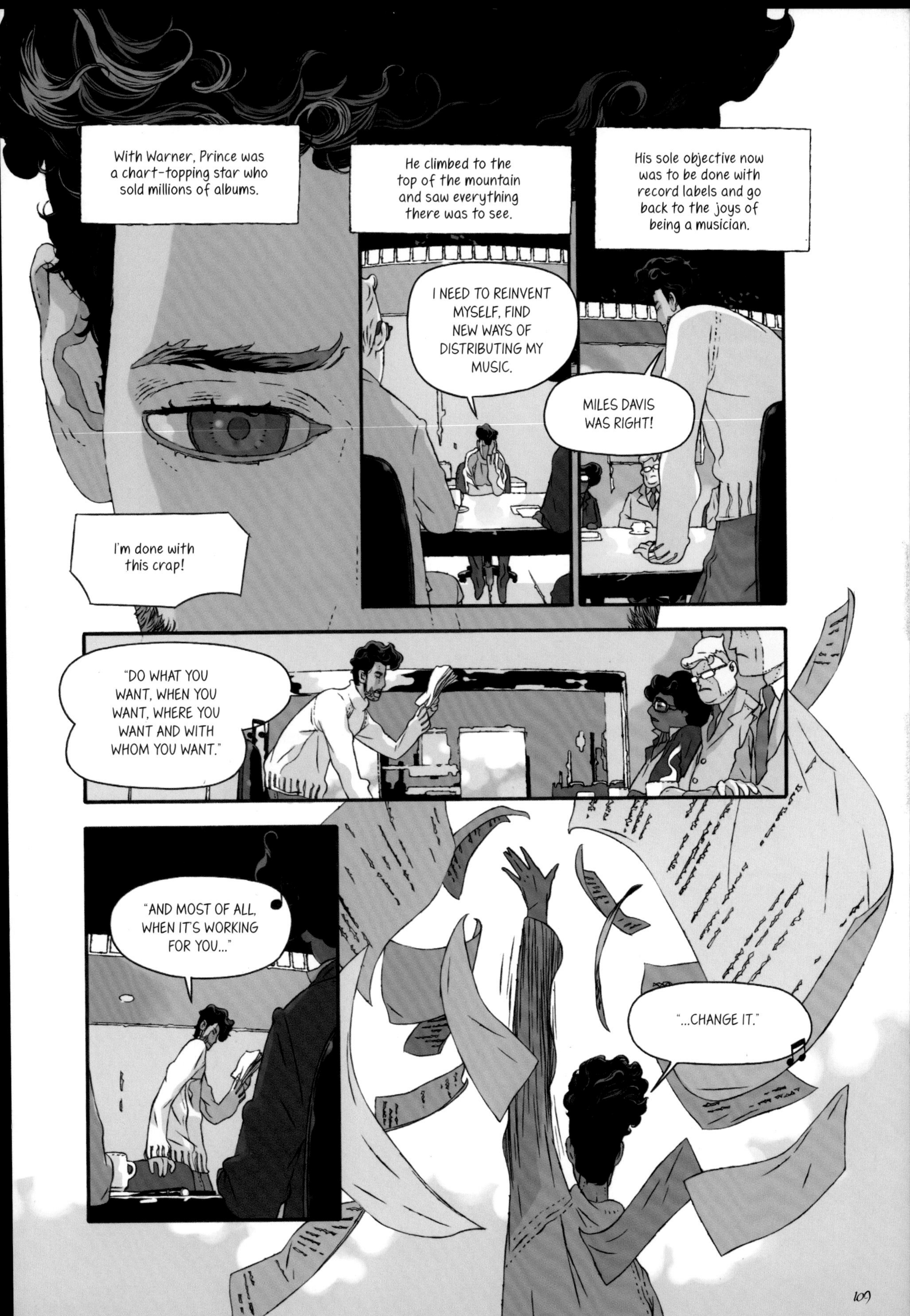
With Warner, Prince was a chart-topping star who sold millions of albums.
He climbed to the top of the mountain and saw everything there was to see.
His sole objective now was to be done with record labels and go back to the joys of being a musician.
I NEED TO REINVENT MYSELF, FIND NEW WAYS OF DISTRIBUTING MY MUSIC.
MILES DAVIS WAS RIGHT!
I'm done with this crap!
"DO WHAT YOU WANT, WHEN YOU WANT, WHERE YOU WANT AND WITH WHOM YOU WANT."
"AND MOST OF ALL, WHEN IT'S WORKING FOR YOU..."
"...CHANGE IT."

By the early 90s, Prince had chosen his strategy: real music by real musicians done live.

He started by opening night clubs called Glam Slam's, where he performed and entertained his network of friends.

First in Minneapolis, of course.

Then in Los Angeles and Miami.

GREAT IDEA, THAT'LL BE AWESOME!

YOU COULD EVEN BROADCAST YOUR SHOWS LIVE BY SATELLITE FROM ONE GLAM SLAM TO ANOTHER.

The concept even traveled all the way to Yokohama, Japan.

In 1993, he explored alternative means of expression, such as Glam Slam Ulysses, a musical show so outrageous and sexually provocative as to make Heidi Fleiss herself blush.*

*KNOWN AS THE HOLLYWOOD MADAM, WHO RAN AN UPSCALE PROSTITUTION RING IN LOS ANG

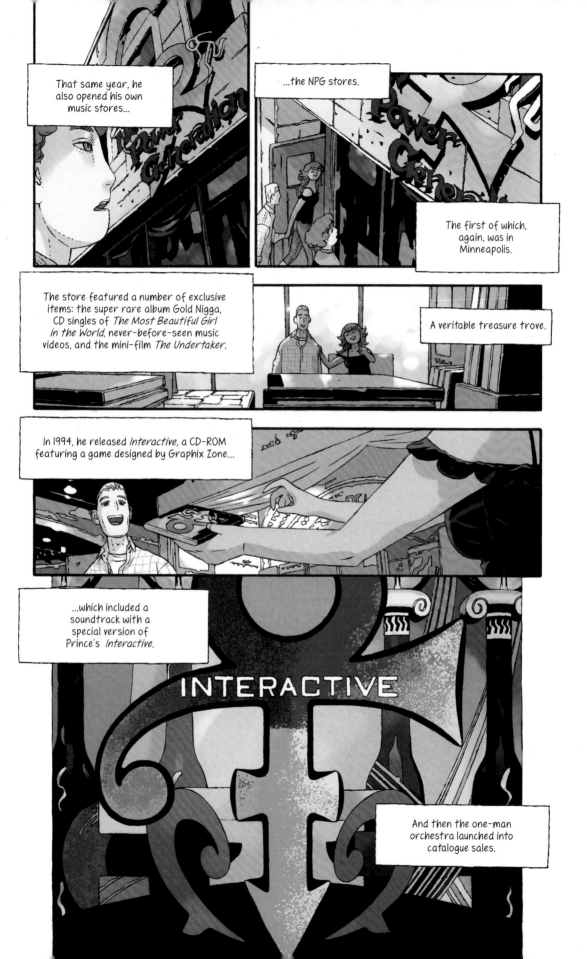

That same year, he also opened his own music stores...

...the NPG stores.

The first of which, again, was in Minneapolis.

The store featured a number of exclusive items: the super rare album Gold Nigga, CD singles of *The Most Beautiful Girl in the World*, never-before-seen music videos, and the mini-film *The Undertaker*.

A veritable treasure trove.

In 1994, he released *Interactive*, a CD-ROM featuring a game designed by Graphix Zone...

...which included a soundtrack with a special version of Prince's *Interactive*.

INTERACTIVE

And then the one-man orchestra launched into catalogue sales.

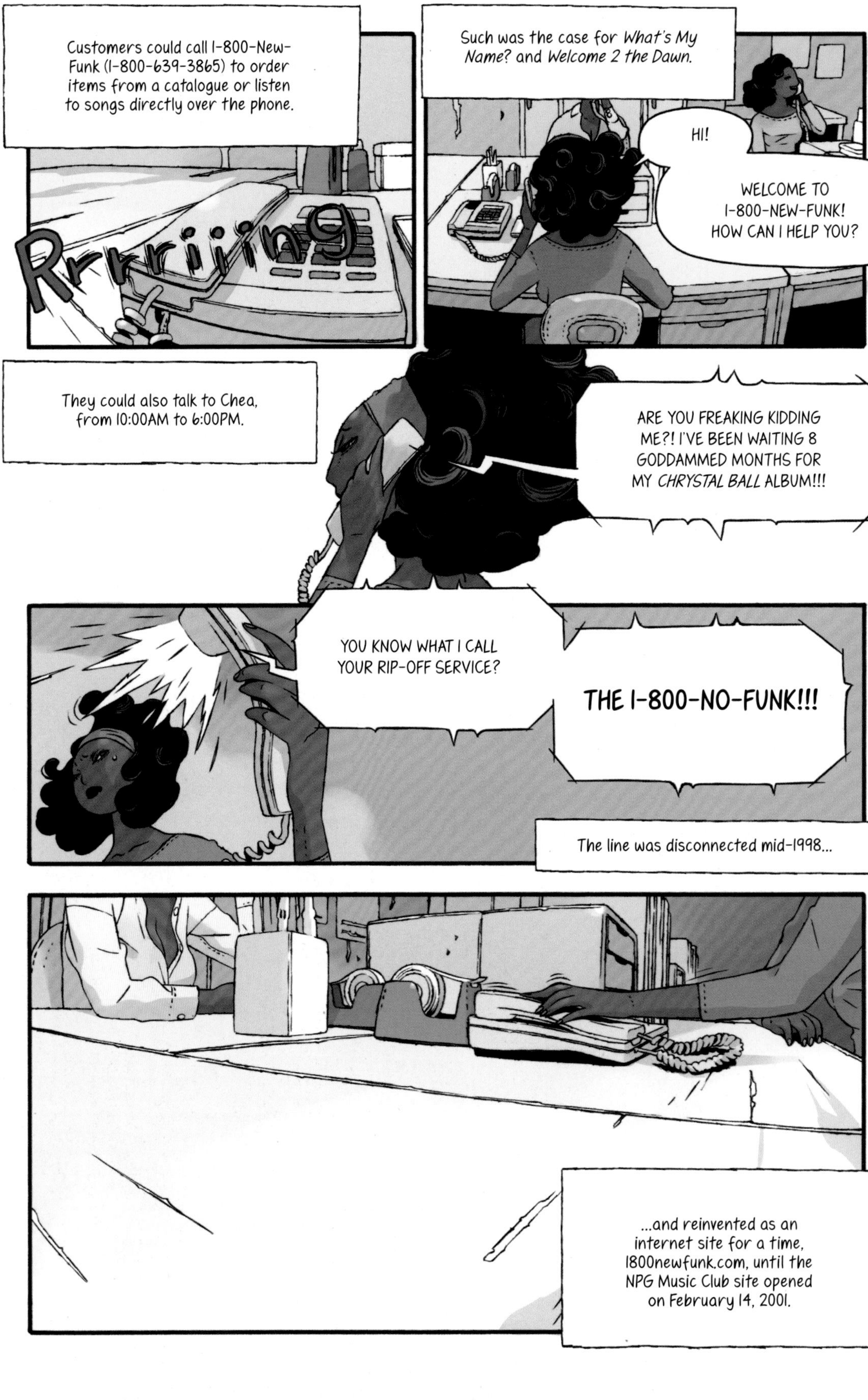

Customers could call 1-800-New-Funk (1-800-639-3865) to order items from a catalogue or listen to songs directly over the phone.
Rrrriiing
Such was the case for *What's My Name?* and *Welcome 2 the Dawn.*
HI!
WELCOME TO 1-800-NEW-FUNK! HOW CAN I HELP YOU?
They could also talk to Chea, from 10:00AM to 6:00PM.
ARE YOU FREAKING KIDDING ME?! I'VE BEEN WAITING 8 GODDAMMED MONTHS FOR MY *CHRYSTAL BALL* ALBUM!!!
YOU KNOW WHAT I CALL YOUR RIP-OFF SERVICE?
THE 1-800-NO-FUNK!!!
The line was disconnected mid-1998...
...and reinvented as an internet site for a time, 1800newfunk.com, until the NPG Music Club site opened on February 14, 2001.

Browsing www.npgmusicclub.com was like visiting a mansion.

WITH THIS SUBSCRIPTION SYSTEM, FANS CAN DOWNLOAD MUSIC AND BUY ALBUMS AND CONCERT TICKETS.

ALSO A GOOD WAY TO PROMOTE SOUNDCHECKS AND AFTERPARTIES.

Online shopping was still new then, but despite a few technical snags and delivery issues, the site managed to attract 400,000 subscribers.

A success that made the "NPGMC" and its content a major aspect of Prince's career.

By taking seemingly crazy chances, the star often left his fans baffled, while regaling them even more with his audacity.

It was a smart move for Prince to draw inspiration from his mentor...

...Miles Davis.

A perpetually unresolved conflict with Warner, artistic forays and the tragedy of losing a child: Prince went through the mid-1990s like one does an ordeal, a punishment. The death of little Amiir at the end of 1996 sounded the death knell for his relationship with Mayte Garcia – especially since she got pregnant again after the loss of their baby and had a miscarriage, which drove the final nail into the coffin of it. Prince would be marked by Amiir's tragic fate for the rest of his life (in *Sex in the Summer*, the first track of the second album in the triple album *Emancipation*, he used the sonogram heartbeats of the fetus as a rhythmic element in the background, as he shared on the *Oprah Winfrey Show*) even though he didn't harbor any hard feelings towards Mayte, to whom he pays

AFTER A TRYING TIME IN HIS LIFE, PRINCE PULLED HIMSELF TOGETHER. DRIVEN BY INEXHAUSTIBLE INSPIRATION, HE EMBARKED ON A SERIES OF ALBUMS AND CONCERTS AT THE TURN OF THE NEW MILLENNIUM THAT REMAIN FOREVER ENGRAVED IN THE MEMORIES OF HIS AUDIENCE.

tribute in *Friend, Lover, Sister, Mother / Wife*, in particular.

But life goes on and the Kid, like everyone else in such a case, set out to rebuild himself, even though life had dealt him a few hard knocks. Work played a central role here. And Prince had a *lot* of work to do! Sure enough: the year 1997, for the artist and his New Power Generation, would be the year of a huge and intense U.S. tour, the Jam of the Year Tour, which would become, by its scope, Prince's biggest U.S. tour ever. A total of ninety-two dates from July 21, 1997 to January 23, 1998, with two August escapades to Calgary and Vancouver, Canada. Symbolically, the Jam of the Year Tour kicked off in the cradle of the blues in Clarksdale, Mississippi, where John Lee Hooker, Sam Cooke, Ike Turner, Muddy Waters and so many other major Black music artists had come from. The concert attracted an audience of just over 14,500, i.e. almost the entire population of the city!

In addition to its supersized scope, one of the tour's great achievements was that it managed to fill venues. 16,000 spectators in Houston, 18,000 in Kansas City, 19,000

Prince on stage in 1999 during the awards ceremony of the NAACP, the National Association for the Advancement of Colored People

At the turn of the 2000s, Prince was one of the first musical artists to embrace the shift to new technologies: CD Rom, internet, etc.

in Nashville, 20,000 in Phoenix, 25,000 in Fargo, etc. – not to mention the after shows, which so many fans were fond of. Apart from the satisfaction of confirming that Prince was still hugely popular, it was also a success from a business standpoint: rather than delegating the organization of the tour to an agent or a professional tour promoter, Prince entrusted it to his own team at Paisley Park. Removing the middlemen greatly increased the profitability of the Jam of the Year Tour, which brought in over 30 million dollars in revenue, according to several sources. In the wake of this obvious resurgence in popularity, two new Prince albums were released almost simultaneously in 1998, still bearing the unpronounceable acronym chosen by the Kid to mark the end of the Warner era. *Crystal Ball* was a quadruple album offering, on the one hand, three albums of rare or previously unreleased titles from the artist's past productions; and on the other hand, an acoustic album, *The Truth*. There was even a limited edition of the album containing, in addition to the aforementioned, a fifth instrumental album, *Kamasutra. Crystal Ball* would be followed five months later by *Newpower Soul*, which marked the end of Prince's collaboration with the band New Power Generation, whose formation had changed many times in the meantime. Talk about productivity! And there's more: at the end of the following year, in 1999, another new album came out, whose 17 tracks were produced by Prince almost entirely alone: *Rave Un2 the Joy Fantastic*. The album was also the fruit of a new contract with another record label, Arista

Records, which allowed the artist to recover the use of his stage name. Phew, the era of the unpronounceable acronym was finally over... Lastly, this period of personal and artistic renewal materialized in 2000 with the creation of a website where fans could listen to new songs online – NPGOnlineLdt. com, which would become NPGmusicclub. com the following year – at a time when this method of distributing music was still largely in its infancy. Prince was thus one of the very first musical artists, along with David Bowie and a few others, to take the risk of investing in this new medium known as the Internet.

No question about it: the Kid was definitely back in the game.

1999
THE VAULT... OLD FRIENDS 4 SALE

1999
RAVE UN2 THE JOY FANTASTIC

AS GOD IS MY WITNESS...

After the artistic rebirth, the spiritual rebirth. Now that his career has been rebooted, Prince broadens his quest in search of meaning in his life. And he lets Larry Graham, a musician who accompanies him and whom he admires, talk him into joining Jehovah's Witnesses. This period of his life coincides with the release of a new album, *The Rainbow Children*, and a new, more intimate format for his concerts.

ART: Noémie Honein

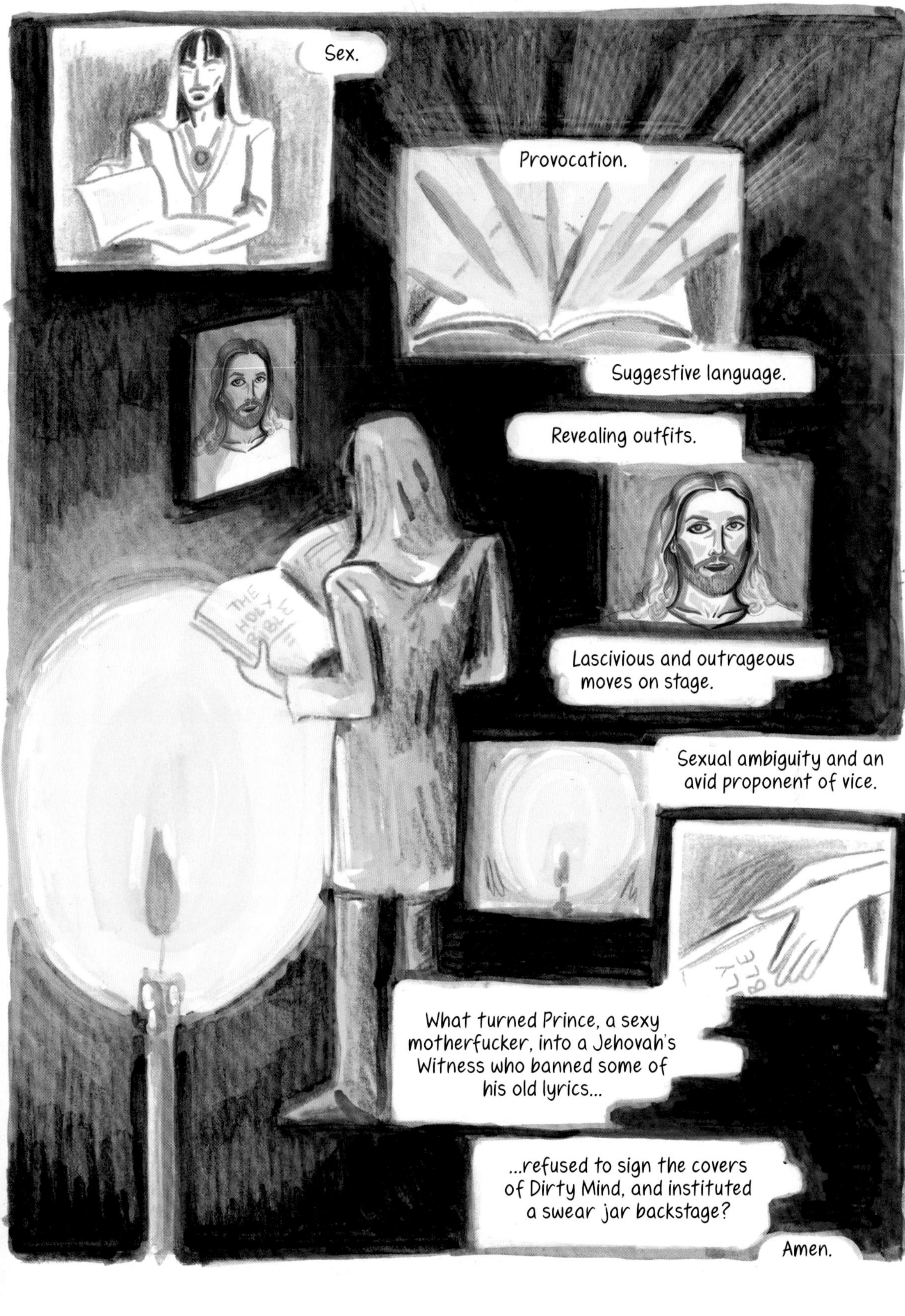
Sex.
Provocation.
Suggestive language.
Revealing outfits.
Lascivious and outrageous moves on stage.
Sexual ambiguity and an avid proponent of vice.
What turned Prince, a sexy motherfucker, into a Jehovah's Witness who banned some of his old lyrics...
...refused to sign the covers of Dirty Mind, and instituted a swear jar backstage?
Amen.

Larry Graham shook up the history of pop twice.

The first time, by banging on the neck of his bass to extract percussions and melodies from it, thereby inventing the "slap" technique.

Countless bass players have imitated the man who, on stage...

... used to hold his instrument up to the heavens like Moses did the Tablets of the Law.

The second time, a few years later, when he inspired one of his admirers to convert into a Jehovah's Witness...

...Prince.

Larry Graham
Blessed be thy name!

The two stars ran into each other
one evening in Nashville, in 1997.

Larry's band, Graham Central Station, was playing
in a suburban venue along with Teena Marie and Earth, Wind & Fire...

...while Prince was crushing it at the Nashville Arena.

After their respective concerts,
Prince invited Larry to an afterparty
in a club downtown...

...before asking him to
open for him on tour.

They've been
together ever since.

The two friends met every night to talk about the Bible.

Jesus Christ never approved the idea that several paths lead to salvation. On the contrary, he said, "For small is the gate and narrow the way leading to life, and few are those who find it." Jehovah's Witnesses believe they have found that path. Otherwise...

...they would be looking for another.

"Toc Toc Toc"

LARRY, I WANT YOU TO TEACH ME THE HOLY SCRIPTURES AND MOVE TO MINNEAPOLIS, NEXT TO MY HOUSE.

I WANT TO BE BAPTIZED.

HELLO, I'M BROTHER NELSON.

PRINCE, THE MASTER OF MYSTERY AND AMBIGUITY, HAD LONG HAD A CAREER TORN BETWEEN SEX AND FAITH.

ARE... ARE YOU... MR.... MR. PRINCE?

THE HOLY BIBLE

Until the dawn of the new millennium, when the kid finally found refuge in a father. A spiritual one.

f all the musicians who worked with Prince throughout his prolific career, some, like Sheila E. and a few others, were more than mere sidekicks. Such was the case in particular of Larry Graham, the great bass player from the legendary band Sly and the Family Stone (which Prince revered) and later the frontman in the 1970s of his own band, Graham Central Station, whose name inspired the name of Prince's first band, Grand Central. In the late 1990s, Graham opened for several Prince concerts, and then, for a time, joined the formation that accompanied him on stage. This closeness between the two artists, no doubt reinforced by an emotional bond akin to a father-son relationship (Graham was born in Texas in 1946, twelve years before Prince), would lead the older musician to talk to his younger brother about his religion. Graham was a Jehovah's Witness, a Christian denomination born in the United States in the 19th century. Today it boasts around eight million followers. A very conservative faith seen as patriarchal and homophobic, Jehovah's Witnesses is often accused of anti-Semitism and pedophilia.

And yet it was this religious movement that Prince, under the obvious influence of Graham, chose to officially join in 2001. This came as quite a surprise for anyone who remembered the often provocative, ambiguous and even transgressive demonstrations of sexual display that the Kid put on during his lengthy career. Then again, perhaps it *wasn't* really all that surprising, since one may also recall the deep quest for spirituality which, beyond perfunctory postures, had always been one of the essential markers of this tortured soul.

Either way, stimulated by this new important stage in his life, Prince kicked off a new world tour in 2002, which his fans had been eagerly awaiting. For at the time, it had been four years since he had toured internationally – an eternity for this natural born performer. The focus of the tour was his critically acclaimed new album, *The Rainbow Children*.

On this occasion, the Kid decided to experiment with a new concert formula: highly polished performances in acoustic and visual terms, put on in small theater-type venues with a maximum seating capacity of just a few thousand, and in a very intimate jazzy, even minimalist register, which he had never tested before. A few carefully selected guest stars joined him on occasion – Larry Graham of course, Sheila E., and Norah Jones among others – but he was also frequently alone on

> **THE SEARCH FOR MEANING IN LIFE HAD ALWAYS BEEN AT THE HEART OF PRINCE'S PERSONALITY. HIS ENCOUNTER WITH THE JEHOVAH'S WITNESSES FAITH CRYSTALLIZED HIS INTENSE NEED FOR SPIRITUALITY.**

Larry Graham (above), a friend of Prince, who had long admired him. Bass players everywhere have Graham to thank for the invention of the slap technique.

FLANDERS EXPO - GENT/GAND
MAANDAG 28 DECEMBRE 98 TE 20.30 U
LUNDI DECEMBER À H
INTERNATIONAL CONCERT ORGANISATION A/S & MAKE IT HAPPEN PROUDLY PRESENTS

THE ARTIST
& NEW POWER GENERATION
SPECIAL GUEST: LARRY GRAHAM

1450 BEF

MAKE IT HAPPEN

stage, at the piano. Taking place over ten months from March to December 2002 successively in the United States, Canada and Europe, the One Nite Alone...Tour gave the artist the opportunity to further grow his audience. **The tour would also result in Prince's first official live album, a sober triple album titled *One Nite Alone...Live!*, released the same year.**

2002
ONE NITE ALONE... LIVE!

2004 - 2006

THE COMEBACK

Prince is back! His new album *Musicology* is a hit and embodies in everyone's eyes a sort of return to grace that his fans hope will be a lasting one. Around the same time, his dazzling stage performance at the Rock and Roll Hall of Fame, in tribute to George Harrison and before his peers, seems to confirm that the Kid is back and that he intends to keep it that way for a long time.

ART: Samuel Figuière

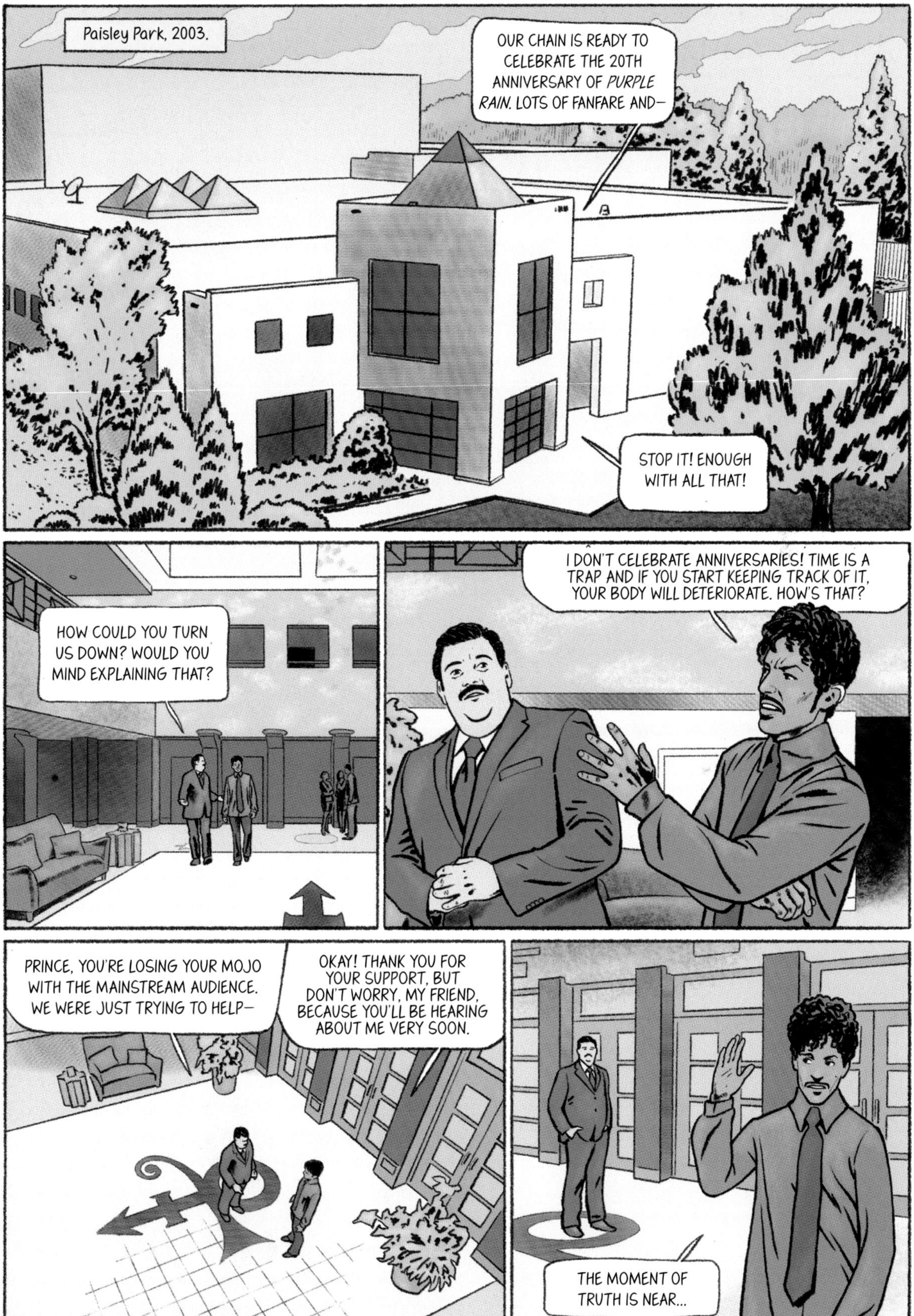
Paisley Park, 2003.
OUR CHAIN IS READY TO CELEBRATE THE 20TH ANNIVERSARY OF PURPLE RAIN. LOTS OF FANFARE AND–
STOP IT! ENOUGH WITH ALL THAT!
HOW COULD YOU TURN US DOWN? WOULD YOU MIND EXPLAINING THAT?
I DON'T CELEBRATE ANNIVERSARIES! TIME IS A TRAP AND IF YOU START KEEPING TRACK OF IT, YOUR BODY WILL DETERIORATE. HOW'S THAT?
PRINCE, YOU'RE LOSING YOUR MOJO WITH THE MAINSTREAM AUDIENCE. WE WERE JUST TRYING TO HELP–
OKAY! THANK YOU FOR YOUR SUPPORT, BUT DON'T WORRY, MY FRIEND, BECAUSE YOU'LL BE HEARING ABOUT ME VERY SOON.
THE MOMENT OF TRUTH IS NEAR...

Losing his "mojo"? That's underestimating Prince.
With *Musicology*, he hits the jackpot at every level.

WHO WAS THAT?

HE OWNS STORES.

WELL?

Sure enough: in typical Prince fashion, he's
preparing a musicians' album for true music lovers.

THE ENTIRE STAFF LOVED YOUR IDEA, BOSS.

But it was also a simple and accessible album, with
an original, well-oiled marketing campaign behind it.

BY INCLUDING THE PRICE OF THE ALBUM IN THE PRICE OF THE CONCERT...

...AND BY HANDING OUT THE ALBUMS BEFORE EACH SHOW, YOU'RE PULLING THE PR STUNT OF THE CENTURY!

I FIRMLY BELIEVE THAT CDS ARE DEAD.

CONCERTS ARE NO LONGER ABOUT PROMOTING A NEW ALBUM. IT'S JUST THE OPPOSITE. THE CONCERT IS THE MAIN EVENT...

...AND THE ALBUM AN ACCESSORY.

The tracks *Call My Name* and *Musicology* land Prince Grammy nominations.

The Musicology Tour is huge and album sales are excellent.

This enables him to renovate the Paisley Park studios and rent a villa in Los Angeles, at 3121 Mulholland Drive...

...where he throws parties for his friends.

TAKE ME TO IT, I'LL PUT A LITTLE AMBIANCE IN HERE!

HA HA! WHO WOULDN'T LET STEVIE WONDER USE THEIR PIANO?

Initially just an address, 3121 began to mean a vibe...

SALMA HAYEK... JUDE LAW.

HI.

...then a concept...

..and lastly an album that went straight to the top of the chart as No. 1 Album on the US Billboard 200.

That had never happened before...

...not even with *Purple Rain.*

Moving once again from a smaller fan base to mainstream appeal, Prince then had another idea...

...a world tour...without traveling!

Indeed, to celebrate Planet Earth, the Earth Tour took place at a single venue: the O2 Arena in London.

In reference to his L.A. address 3121, he played 21 shows, through September 21, with tickets costing 31.21£.

All 21 shows at the 20,000-seat venue sold out! A veritable marathon reinforced by 13 aftershows at the IndigO2, a 2,000-seat venue located on the same property as the O2!

You do the math: for that series of concerts, and without ever leaving the city, Prince attracted 400,000 fans from around the world through nothing but his pure genius.

"Losing my mojo," the guy said. Yeah, *right*.

Was it the newfound faith with which he was overflowing? Was it finding favor with the mainstream audience again? Whatever it was, in 2004, inspiration revisited Prince, as spectacularly evidenced by his new album, released in the spring: *Musicology*. His fans, of course, were onboard at once, and they made the new record a commercial triumph, but it won over the critics, as well, who considered the album to be Prince's best one since *Diamonds and Pearls*--in other words, the best one in almost fifteen years. In fact, it was during this period that the American magazine *Rolling Stone*, still influential at that time, chose to qualify the Kid as the most productive artist in the world. A well-earned title to be sure. But the climax of this year 2004 would remain the breathtaking public performance that Prince gave at the Rock and Roll Hall of Fame, the famed American institution that rewards the heroes of popular music every year. Inducted that year, Prince joined an impressive line-up of musicians on stage for a posthumous tribute to the legendary George Harrison, one of the four Beatles. And it was of course his iconic song *While My Guitar Gently Weeps* that was chosen

IN THE MID-2000S, PRINCE WAS BACK IN FULL FORCE AND TOP FORM. AND HE USED INNOVATIVE APPROACHES TO PROMOTE HIS MUSIC, SUCH AS BY OFFERING CONCERT GOERS HIS NEW CD *MUSICOLOGY*, HIS BEST WORK IN 15 YEARS.

The Rock & Roll Hall of Fame in Cleveland.

Prince and Beyon
stage together
Grammy Awards
Angeles,

for a group performance featuring none less than Tom Petty, Steve Winwood, Jeff Lynne (famous in the U.S. for having led the group Electric Light Orchestra and rubbing shoulders with Bob Dylan, George Harrison, Tom Petty and Roy Orbison in the short-lived "supergroup" The Traveling Wilburys) and Dhani Harrison, George's own son. Heavy hitters, in other words. Except that Prince, who remained in the sha███ during the first three minutes of the ███████ ████ only stepped out int█████ ████████████████████ ████ gu█ f██ i██ i██

2004 with an initiative as original as it was unexpected: to offer the Musicology CD to anyone attending his concerts! This was not the first time, actually, that the artist had used innovative ways to distribute his own work. In the early 1990s, he had launched the NPG Stores, where both his current discography and a few new, unreleased albums were sold; then there was the bold episode of telephone sales, followed a few years later by the distribution of his works via the internet, a truly pioneering initiative at a time when not many musicians had ventured into this new medium.

In 2004, the CD offered to each attendee at the entrance to his concert venues during the Musicology Tour caused a stir. We're talking about 400,000 copies handed out in this way! Which, incidentally, helped change the way album sales were counted, since in this specific case the CDs, the price of which was included in the price of the concert ticket, had in fact been sold, despite appearances to the contrary. **Once again, the Kid managed to take his world by surprise.**

2004
MUSICOLOGY

2007
THE GREATEST SHOW ON EARTH

The mid-2000s saw Prince doing a number of extraordinary shows. In 2007, he performed at the Super Bowl's halftime show for the first time—a show that, to this day, still ranks as the best Super Bowl halftime show of all time on every major list.

ART: Christopher

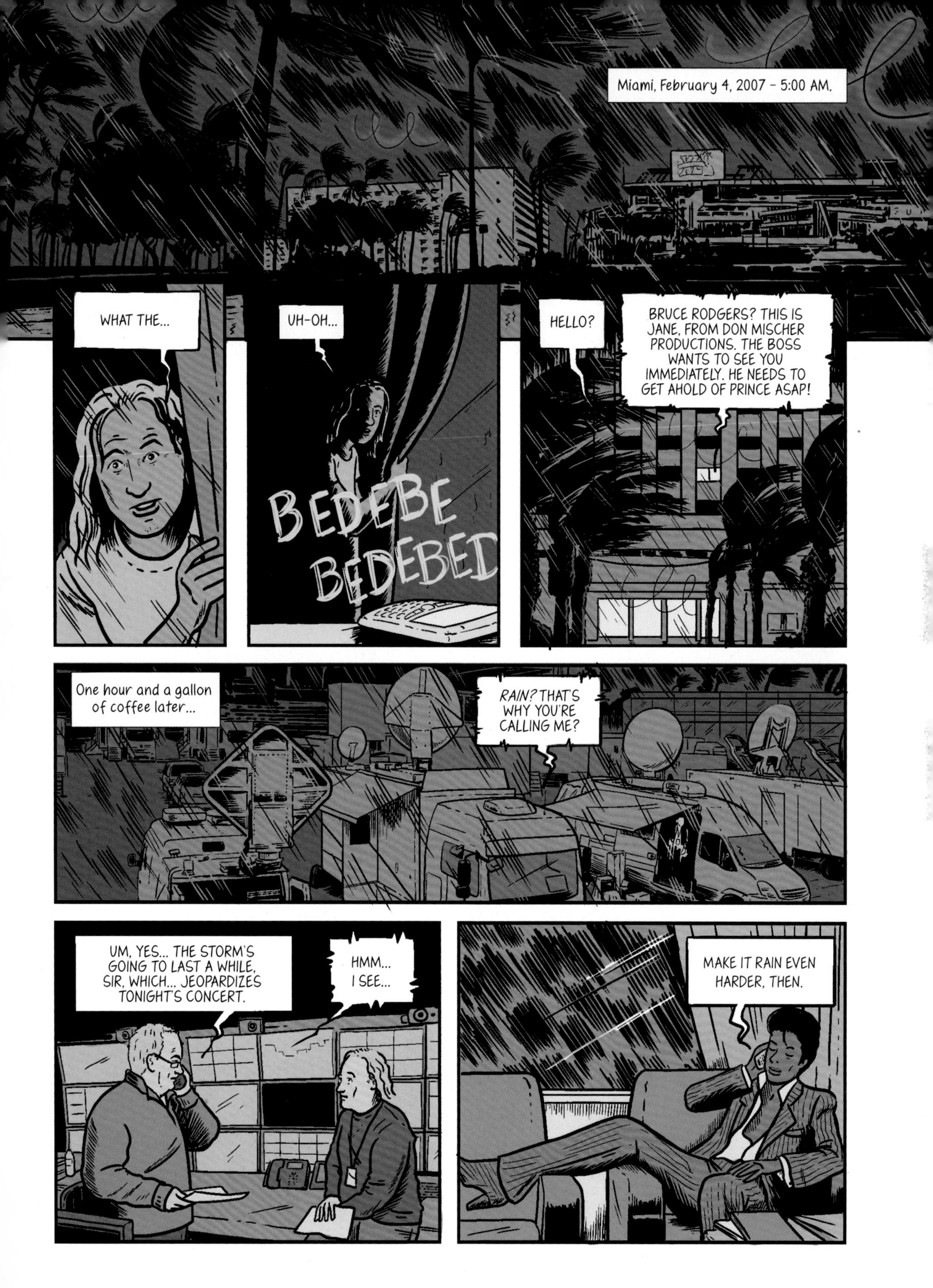

Miami, February 4, 2007 – 5:00 AM.
WHAT THE...
UH-OH...
BEDEBE BEDEBED
HELLO?
BRUCE RODGERS? THIS IS JANE, FROM DON MISCHER PRODUCTIONS. THE BOSS WANTS TO SEE YOU IMMEDIATELY. HE NEEDS TO GET AHOLD OF PRINCE ASAP!
One hour and a gallon of coffee later...
RAIN? THAT'S WHY YOU'RE CALLING ME?
UM, YES... THE STORM'S GOING TO LAST A WHILE, SIR, WHICH... JEOPARDIZES TONIGHT'S CONCERT.
HMM... I SEE...
MAKE IT RAIN EVEN HARDER, THEN.

A few minutes before the Super Bowl Halftime Show.

IT HASN'T RAINED AT THE SUPER BOWL IN 40 YEARS, BRUCE. 40 YEARS!

COME ON, GUYS, IT'S 16-14. LET'S FINISH THIS!

Prince requires four different electric guitars for his live show, and...

"ELECTRIC" IS PRECISELY THE PROBLEM. NOT TO MENTION THE REST OF THE GEAR!

YES, MR. RODGERS. WE'VE SECURED ZONE 3. BUT THE STAGE IS STILL A PADDLING POOL!

OK. IF ANYONE SLIPS, TURN THE CAMERAS AWAY!

WE'RE TAKING A HUGE RISK, DON... A HUMILIATING DISASTER LIVE ON WORLD TV!

WELL, THERE'S NOTHING WE CAN DO NOW, SO....

JUST CROSS ALL YOUR FINGERS AND SAY A PRAYER...

The show started off under thunderclaps...

...then a cover of Queen's *We Will Rock You.*

The rain poured down, hammering the sheet metal of Dolphin Stadium...

The Twins, perched on 8-inch heels, were the most at risk.

The Marching 100 band from Florida A&M University struggled in the downpour...

...while Shelby Johnson did the best she could...

All the conditions were ripe for making the show a spectacular flop.

It would be just the opposite.

Which Prince could predict.

No self-promotion. The star sang his songs, as well as songs by Bob Dylan, Foo Fighters, John Fogerty and others.

When it came time for *Purple Rain*, Mother Nature, Prince's partner in cr[...] for a night, celebrated her prodigy by unleashing on him tons upon tons [...] rain, ever harder. Under the spotlights, the performance became pure mo[...]

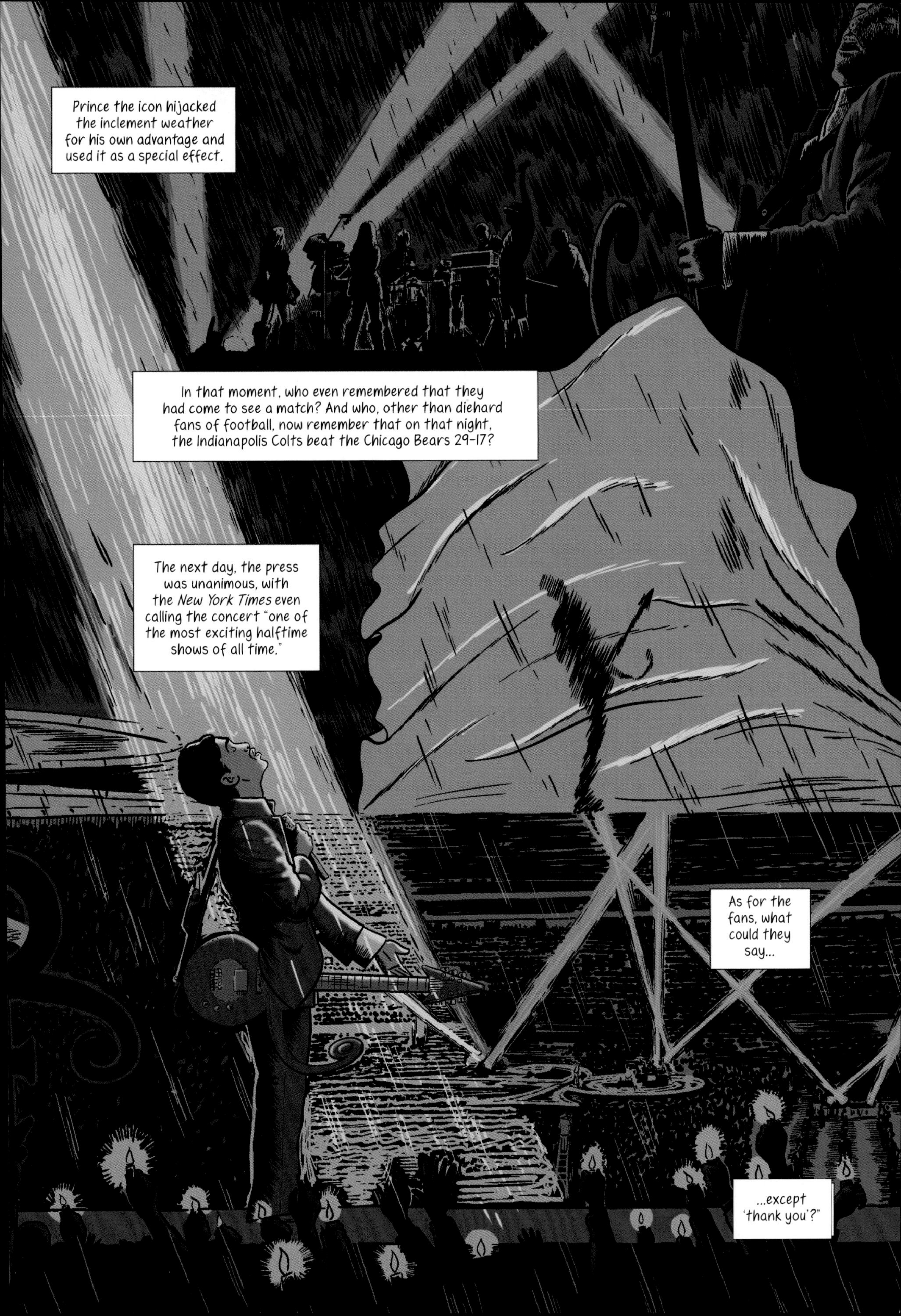
Prince the icon hijacked the inclement weather for his own advantage and used it as a special effect.
In that moment, who even remembered that they had come to see a match? And who, other than diehard fans of football, now remember that on that night, the Indianapolis Colts beat the Chicago Bears 29–17?
The next day, the press was unanimous, with the *New York Times* even calling the concert "one of the most exciting halftime shows of all time."
As for the fans, what could they say...
...except 'thank you'?"

Prince certainly had his share of glorious moments throughout his astonishing career. But not quite like this one... Perhaps you have to be American to fully grasp what the Super Bowl is and represents. It is so much more than a mere football game, it is a unique moment of communion, where people come together on Super Bowl Sunday in bars and at home barbecues and celebrate together what is as much a full sporting event and show as the joy and pride of being in America. The Super Bowl has been held every year since the mid-1960s, usually at the start of the year and each time in a different city, chosen many months in advance. The number of spectators varies according to the capacity of the stadium, but is almost never less than 60,000 and can exceed 103,000, as was the case several times at Rose Bowl Stadium in Pasadena, California. And there's the television audience: the Super Bowl airs in more than 200 countries and attracts at least 100 million viewers every year – primarily in North America. At the heart of this TV event is the half-time show, which is a major draw in itself and has gradually become a tradition. For a long time it featured local marching bands, before giving way, over the years, to big names from the pop and rock world. Michael Jackson was the main act in 1993, as were, over the years, Diana Ross, the New Kids on the Block, ZZ Top, Aerosmith, U2, Paul McCartney, the Rolling Stones, Bruce Springsteen, Madonna, Beyoncé, Lady Gaga and many others.

In 2007, after a career revival following his recent achievements, Prince was chosen as the main act of the half-time show. The event was set for February 4 and it once again took place in Miami, Florida (the city holds the record for the number of Super Bowls hosted there). The Kid's performance at Dolphin Stadium would be more than princely: it would be epic!

Besides the quality of his set list (in chronological order, it was *We Will Rock You* by Queen, *Let's Go Crazy*, *1999*, *Baby I'm a Star*, *Proud Mary* by Creedence Clearwater Revival, *All Along the Watchtower* by Bob Dylan, *Best of You* by Foo Fighters and *Purple Rain* for the finale), Prince galvanized

> **PRINCE'S MAGICAL APPEARANCE AT THE 2007 SUPER BOWL WAS MORE THAN JUST SUCCESSFUL: IT WAS A MOMENT OF GRACE PERFORMED BY AN ARTIST POSSESSED BY MUSIC. THAT EVENING, PRINCE PLAYED IN FRONT OF HIS BIGGEST AUDIENCE EVER.**

The stage at Dolphin Stadium in Miami, Florida, emblazoned with the Prince logo. The city holds the record for the number of Super Bowls hosted there.

new format of concerts in residence in Las Vegas and then in Los Angeles, backed by his freshly released album 3121. He used the same principle again the following year in London, where he put on twenty-one sold-out concerts in a row, in a single venue with a capacity of 18,000 spectators, the O2 Arena. As with *Musicology* three years earlier, all ticket holders received a free copy of his newly released album, in this case Planet Earth. **And he also distributed the album in Great Britain by including it inside a special edition of the weekly paper Mail on Sunday. Circulation: three million...**

the public not only with his masterful performance, but also his courage. Because, as forecast several days earlier by the local weather channels, a major storm raged and torrents of rain fell on the stadium at half-time.

Many other entertainers would have erred on the side of caution and bowed out – and probably no one would have really held it against them. Faced with the unleashed elements, the Kid chose to face them instead and, in the spur of the moment, brought the purple hues of the light show to their maximum intensity as he completed his show with *Purple Rain*. A sequence of pure splendor, served by exceptional circumstances and an artist literally possessed by his art while performing in a downpour...

Prince's performance that night became the stuff of legend. Nearly 75,000 people were in the stadium and some 110 million in front of their television sets. He had never had – and never would have again– such a large audience. Echoing this absolutely extraordinary episode, Prince during this time distinguished himself with public performances that were always unexpected. In 2006, he had launched a

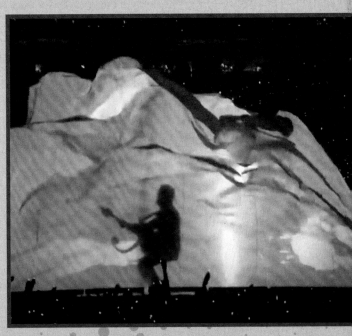

Prince in performance. That evening, amidst a fury of unleashed elements, he does better than surpass himself, he transcends himself.

2009
PRINCE PRODUCER

Forever brimming with ideas, the Kid from Minneapolis found a way to exploit his surplus of creativity early on: entrusting others with the task of developing or performing his newest discoveries as a composer and producer. As such, he played the role of Pygmalion throughout his life, a role he delighted in, especially with women: Prince as inspiration, producer, mentor... and sometimes more.

DESSIN : Kongkee

Los Angeles - Fall 2008.

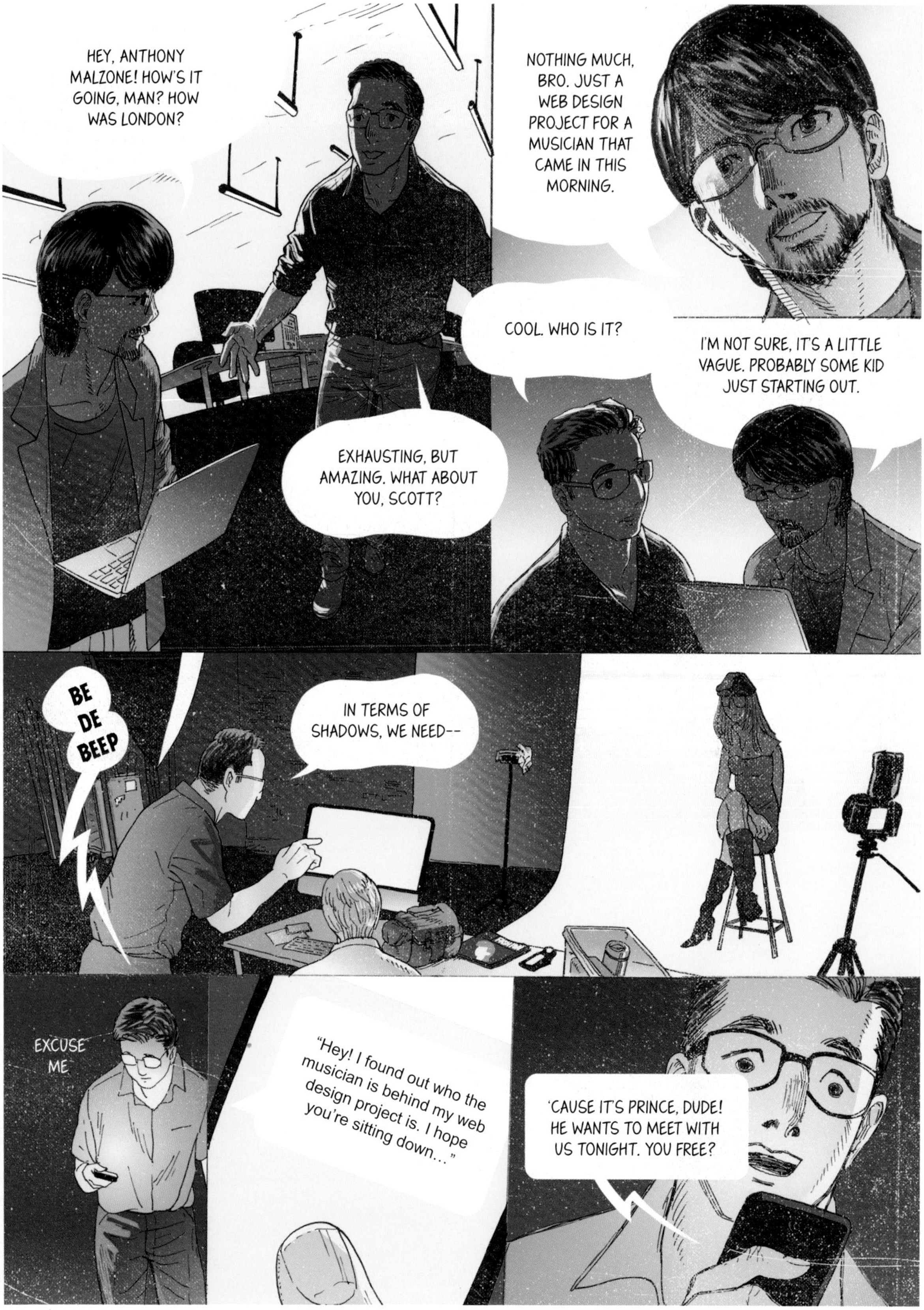
HEY, ANTHONY MALZONE! HOW'S IT GOING, MAN? HOW WAS LONDON?
EXHAUSTING, BUT AMAZING. WHAT ABOUT YOU, SCOTT?
NOTHING MUCH, BRO. JUST A WEB DESIGN PROJECT FOR A MUSICIAN THAT CAME IN THIS MORNING.
COOL. WHO IS IT?
I'M NOT SURE, IT'S A LITTLE VAGUE. PROBABLY SOME KID JUST STARTING OUT.
BE DE BEEP
IN TERMS OF SHADOWS, WE NEED--
EXCUSE ME
"Hey! I found out who the musician is behind my web design project is. I hope you're sitting down..."
'CAUSE IT'S PRINCE, DUDE! HE WANTS TO MEET WITH US TONIGHT. YOU FREE?

77 Beverly Park – That night.

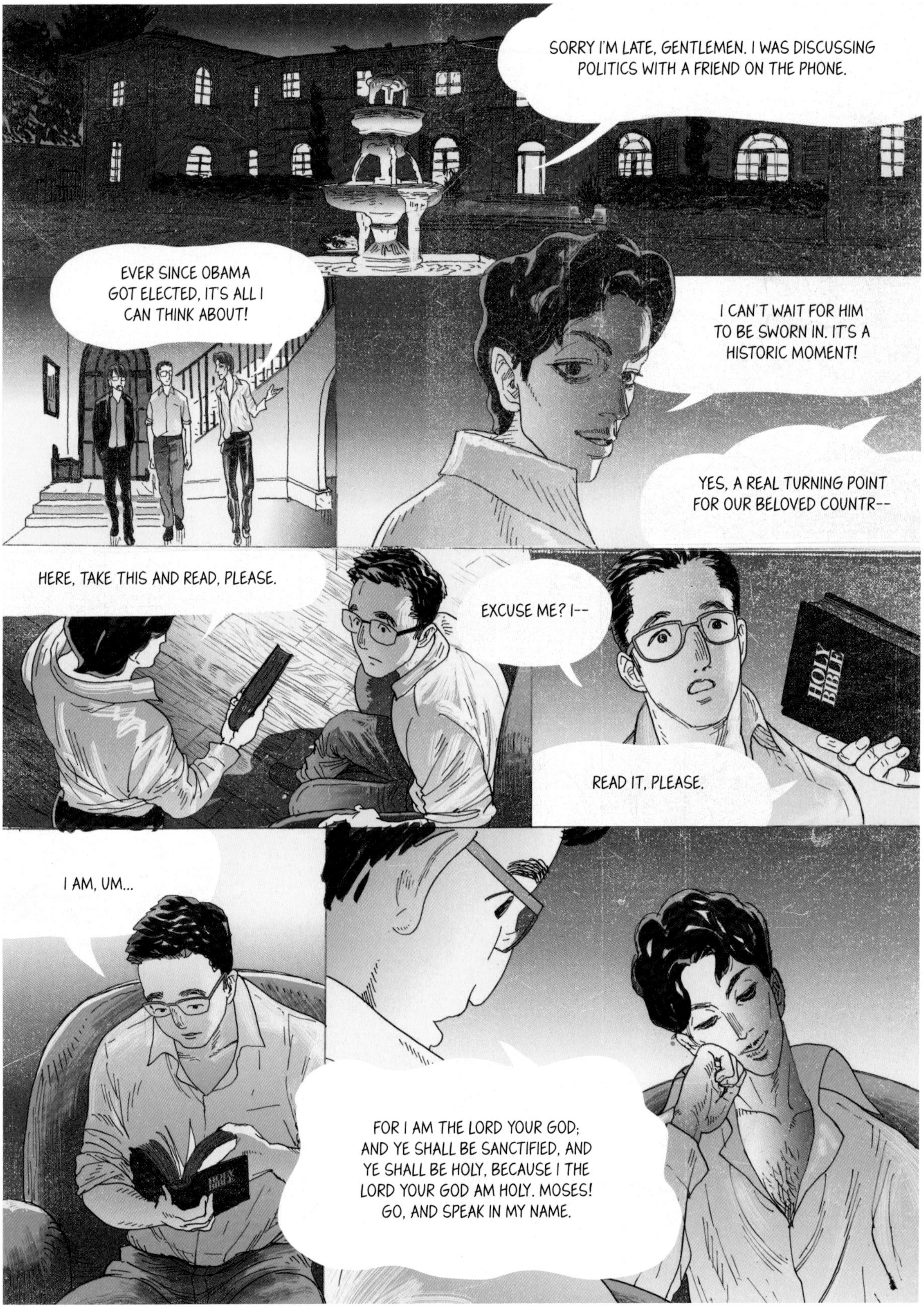
SORRY I'M LATE, GENTLEMEN. I WAS DISCUSSING POLITICS WITH A FRIEND ON THE PHONE.
EVER SINCE OBAMA GOT ELECTED, IT'S ALL I CAN THINK ABOUT!
I CAN'T WAIT FOR HIM TO BE SWORN IN. IT'S A HISTORIC MOMENT!
YES, A REAL TURNING POINT FOR OUR BELOVED COUNTR--
HERE, TAKE THIS AND READ, PLEASE.
EXCUSE ME? I--
HOLY BIBLE
READ IT, PLEASE.
I AM, UM...
HOLY BIBLE
FOR I AM THE LORD YOUR GOD; AND YE SHALL BE SANCTIFIED, AND YE SHALL BE HOLY, BECAUSE I THE LORD YOUR GOD AM HOLY. MOSES! GO, AND SPEAK IN MY NAME.

Three hours of theology, sociology and politics later, Prince finally decides to talk music...

WOW, IT'S GREAT!

CLICK!

THE THREE-WORK BOX SET WILL BE CALLED *LOTUSFLOW3R*...

THANKS.

...AND I NEED YOU TO HELP ME CREATE A WEBSITE TO DISTRIBUTE THEM.

I WANT TO SIGN ARTISTS THAT CAN PROMOTE THEIR OWN "GALAXY" IN A VIRTUAL UNIVERSE. DO YOU UNDERSTAND?

SO...UM... A "COSMIC" FEEL, THEN?

EXACTLY.

I WANT A LABEL LIKE TIDAL,* SO I CAN FIND THE NEW KINGS OF LEON** AND THE NEW *SEX ON FIRE*.***

WE'LL LAUNCH WITH TWO OF MY ALBUMS AND ONE BY BRIA VALENTE, MY LATEST DISCOVERY AND PROTÉGÉE.

KIND OF LIKE SHEILA E., BACK IN THE HEYDAY?

AH! BUT IT WASN'T JUST HER! THERE WAS VANITY, APOLLONIA KOTERO...

*MUSICAL STREAMING PLATFORM
** AMERICAN ALTERNATIVE ROCK BAND.
***A SONG BY KINGS OF LEON.

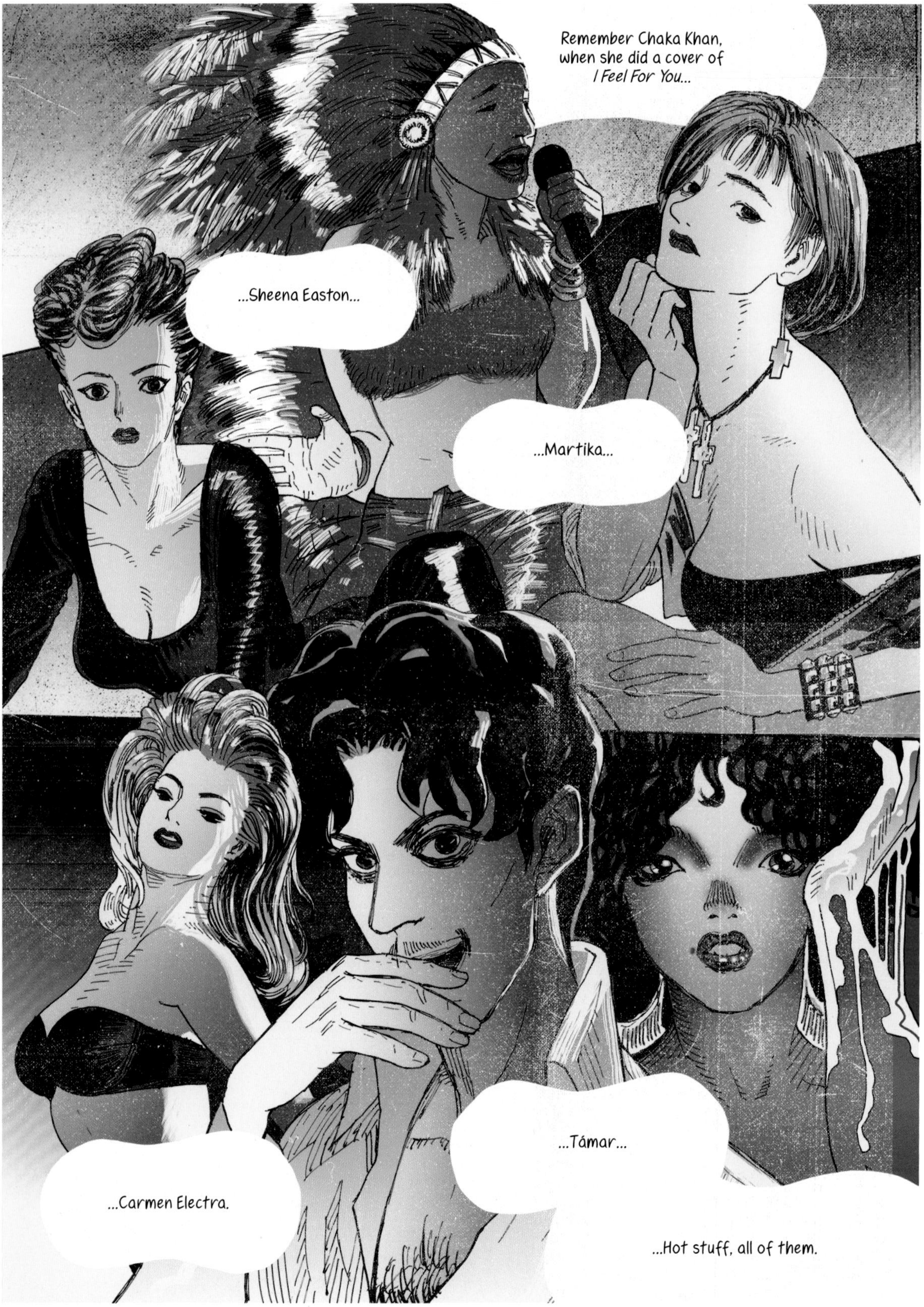
Remember Chaka Khan, when she did a cover of *I Feel For You*...
...Sheena Easton...
...Martika...
...Támar...
...Carmen Electra.
...Hot stuff, all of them.

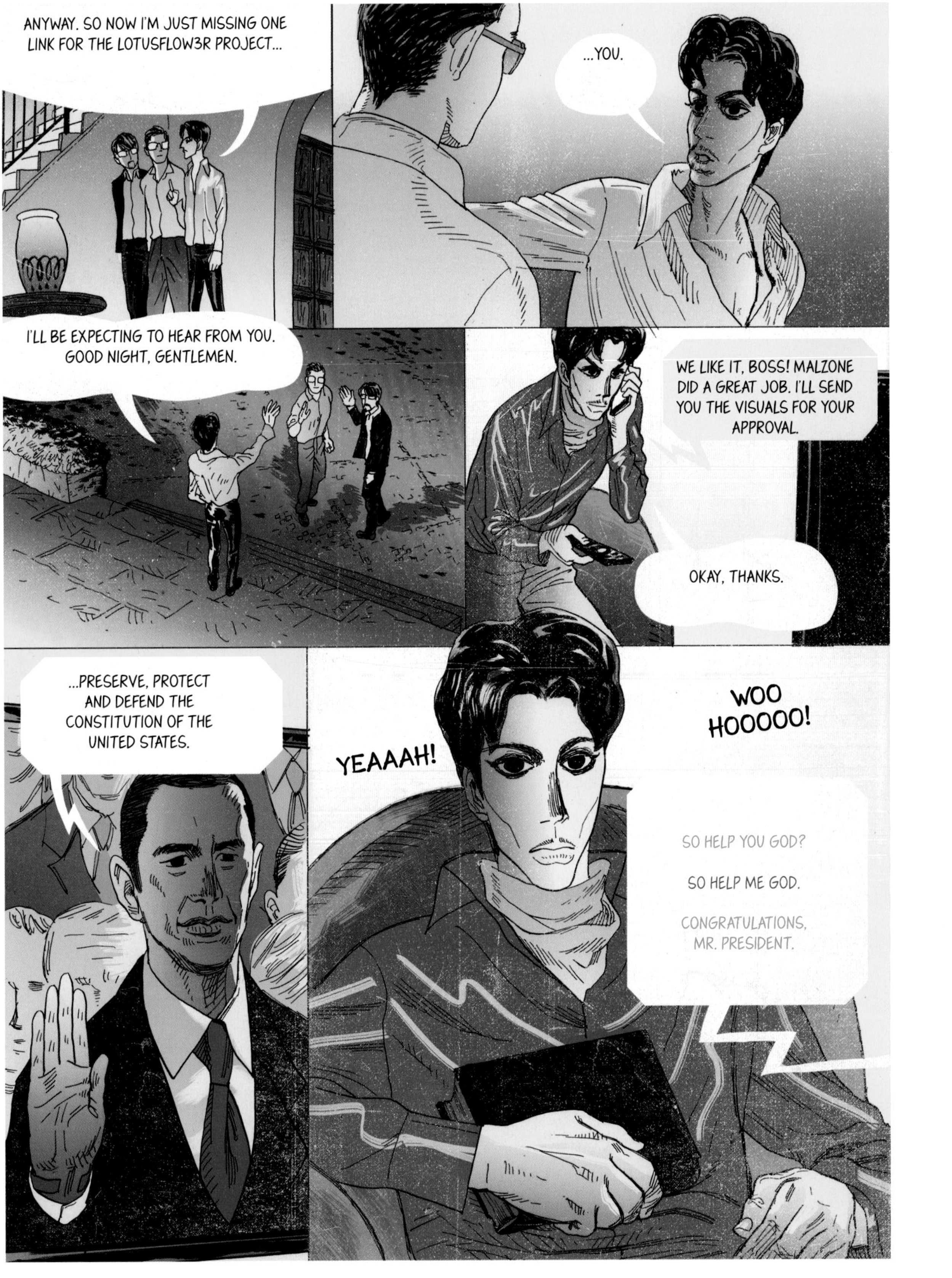
ANYWAY. SO NOW I'M JUST MISSING ONE LINK FOR THE LOTUSFLOW3R PROJECT...
...YOU.
I'LL BE EXPECTING TO HEAR FROM YOU. GOOD NIGHT, GENTLEMEN.
WE LIKE IT, BOSS! MALZONE DID A GREAT JOB. I'LL SEND YOU THE VISUALS FOR YOUR APPROVAL.
OKAY, THANKS.
...PRESERVE, PROTECT AND DEFEND THE CONSTITUTION OF THE UNITED STATES.
YEAAAH!
WOO HOOOOO!
SO HELP YOU GOD?
SO HELP ME GOD.
CONGRATULATIONS, MR. PRESIDENT.

> PRINCE HAD ALWAYS LIVED IN A STATE OF PERMANENT CREATION. THE MANY ARTISTS WITH WHOM HE SURROUNDED HIMSELF AND WHOM HE PRODUCED OR SUPPORTED ENABLED HIM TO BRING TO LIFE THE MUSICAL IDEAS THAT HE HAD NOT BEEN ABLE OR WANTED TO EXPLOIT UNDER HIS OWN NAME.

In the spring of 2009, a new Prince album was announced. As had often been the case since the early 2000s, its title, *Lotusflow3r*, seemed a bit convoluted. And what also didn't come as a surprise to his fans was the generous volume: nothing less than a triple CD. But this new release did actually come with a surprise. One of the album's three CDs, *Elixer*, did not feature songs by Prince, but by an artist who had been his close friend for two years: the singer Bria Valente.

Born Brenda Fuentes, this Minneapolis native had actually already worked with Prince, as a backing vocalist on his 2007 album *Planet Earth*. But this time, her mentor had pushed her into the limelight, and pairing up with Prince on one of his own albums was obviously, from a purely business standpoint, a huge promotional boost. Doing this was yet another example of something the Kid had always loved doing, practically since the start of his career: playing Pygmalion.

As soon as his career took off at the dawn of the 1980s, he had pushed forward the Canadian model Denise Matthews, renamed Vanity (rumor has it that he had first wanted to call her Vagina...) as part of the sexy female group Vanity 6. Vanity having taken off on the eve of the filming of *Purple Rain*, the film, it was another former model, Patricia Apollonia Kotero, who replaced her in the project (and in the arms of princely affection) under the stage name Apollonia. Like Vanity, Apollonia's own career would greatly benefit from her association with the Kid.

Vanity 6, the first of Prince's girl bands. The opposite of a boy band, the trio set the stage on fire wherever they went.

The following years saw many other "favorites" join Prince's inner circle, and in the process benefit from his creativity with regards to promoting, guiding or enriching their personal artistic journey. Sheila E., very talented in her own right, greatly benefited from this relationship, as did another who came after her, Tara Leigh Patrick, aka Carmen Electra – another ex-model – who saw her eponymous album released on the Paisley Park Records label after sometimes opening for Prince on his Diamonds and Pearls Tour. Mayte Garcia, who worked with him as a dancer

and backing vocalist several years, would probably have followed the same path if the tragedy of their child's death had not abruptly put an end to their relationship as a couple and their artistic collaboration. There would be many more artists in Prince's trophy case as a producer, without whom he wasn't necessarily romantically involved. Some examples: the Scottish singer Sheena Easton, his very convincing co-star on the powerful *U Got the Look* on the album *Sign 'o the Times*; the singer and poet Ingrid Chavez, who took part in the film *Graffiti Bridge*; and Irish singer Sinéad O'Connor, who turned the song *Nothing Compares 2 U* into a hit. Others would follow over time. There were "protégées" with whom the nature of their relationship with the Kid was not always clearly known, such as Tamar (Ashley Tamar Davis) and the Cameroonian singer Andy Allo, as well as bands and individual artists whom Prince produced and/or composed for and who were as varied as the Bangles, a small hit band from the 1980s that has been somewhat forgotten today, Chaka Khan, Mavis Staples, George Clinton and Maceo Parker. **And some say that man didn't make his mark?**

Some of Prince's performers over the years. From left to right and top to bottom Carmen Electra, Bria Valente and Sinéad O'Connor.

2009
LOTUSFLOW3R

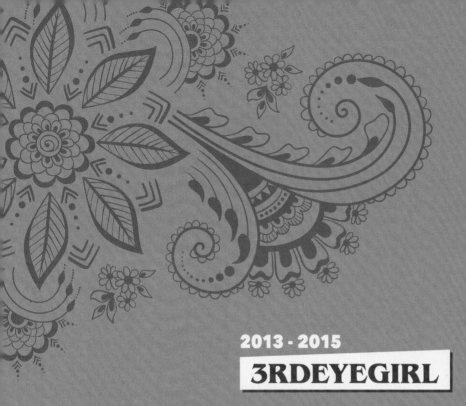

2013 · 2015

3RDEYEGIRL

Having gone through countless musical incarnations over the course of an artistic journey unlike any other, in 2013, Prince chooses to return to one of his fundamentals: rock! And he once again takes his world by surprise by recruiting an amateur band made up of three fearless girls. 3rdeyegirl killed it alongside the master, and proved to the skeptics, just in case there were still any left, that the Minneapolis Kid still knew how to take his act to unexpected places.

ART: Léah Touitou

THE YEAR WAS 2012. I WAS PLAYING IN A CLUB WHEN I WAS APPROACHED BY A GUY WHO SAID HE REPRESENTED A "BIG ARTIST."

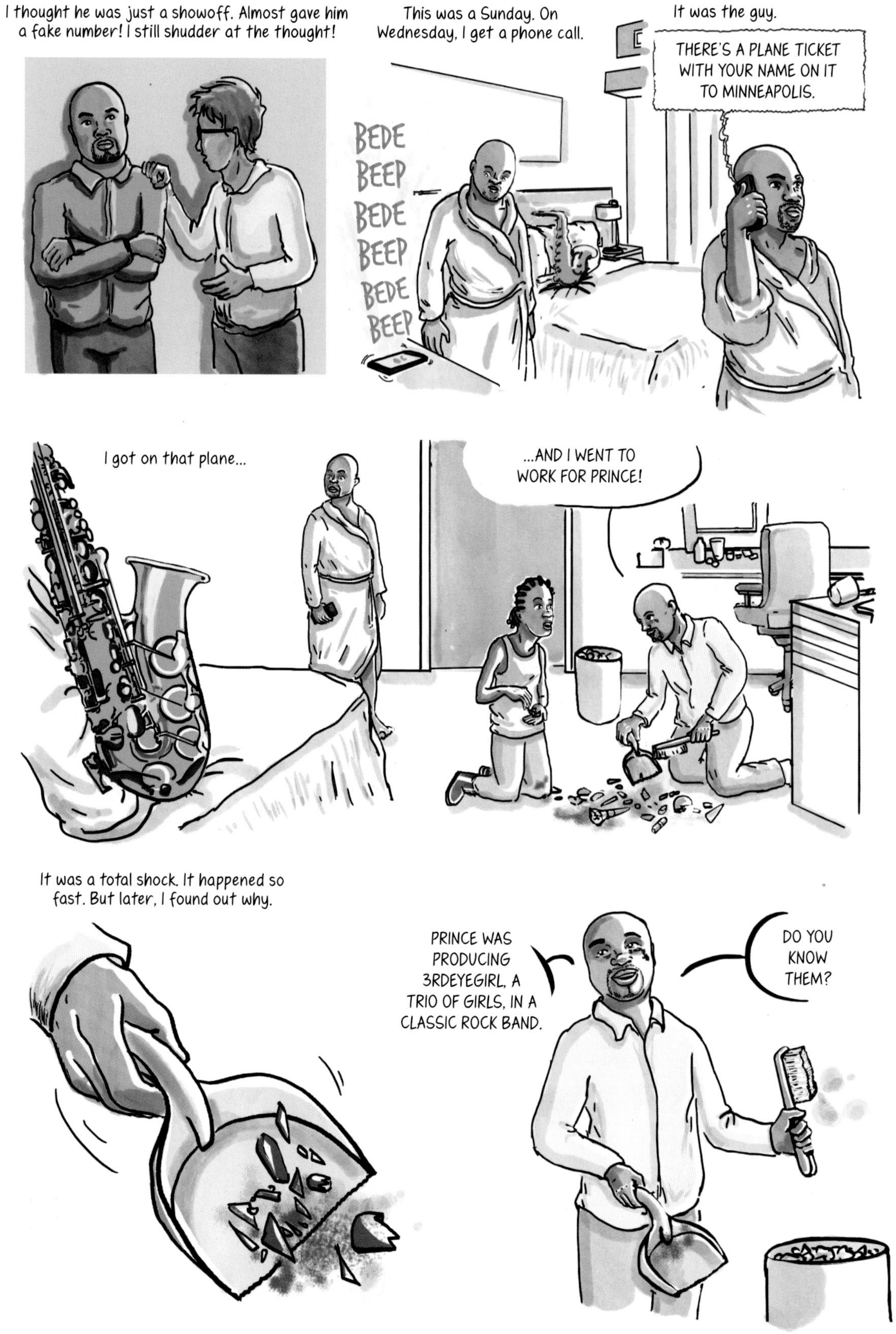
I thought he was just a showoff. Almost gave him a fake number! I still shudder at the thought!
This was a Sunday. On Wednesday, I get a phone call.
BEDE BEEP BEDE BEEP BEDE BEEP
It was the guy.
THERE'S A PLANE TICKET WITH YOUR NAME ON IT TO MINNEAPOLIS.
I got on that plane...
...AND I WENT TO WORK FOR PRINCE!
It was a total shock. It happened so fast. But later, I found out why.
PRINCE WAS PRODUCING 3RDEYEGIRL, A TRIO OF GIRLS, IN A CLASSIC ROCK BAND.
DO YOU KNOW THEM?

Hannah Ford-Welton on drums.

Donna Grantis on guitar.

And Ida Nielsen on base.

It was great but not great enough. He also wanted a brass section with Maceo Parker, Trombone Shorty, and me.

And then...

...HE CHANGED HIS MIND. IT ENDED UP BEING 11 OF US! HIS LARGEST BRASS SECTION EVER!

It was nuts. He would explain what he wanted, we played, and he'd spend the night mixing it himself.

One day, during a group session...

TELL ME, GUYS, WHO'S YOUR FAVORITE SAX PLAYER?

JOHN COLTRANE!

"CANNONBALL" ADDERLEY!

SIDNEY BECHET!

ME, I'D SAY IT'S MARCUS HERE!

I burst out laughing at the thought of it. Me, a humble jazzman from North Carolina!

WHAT'S SO FUNNY, MARCUS?

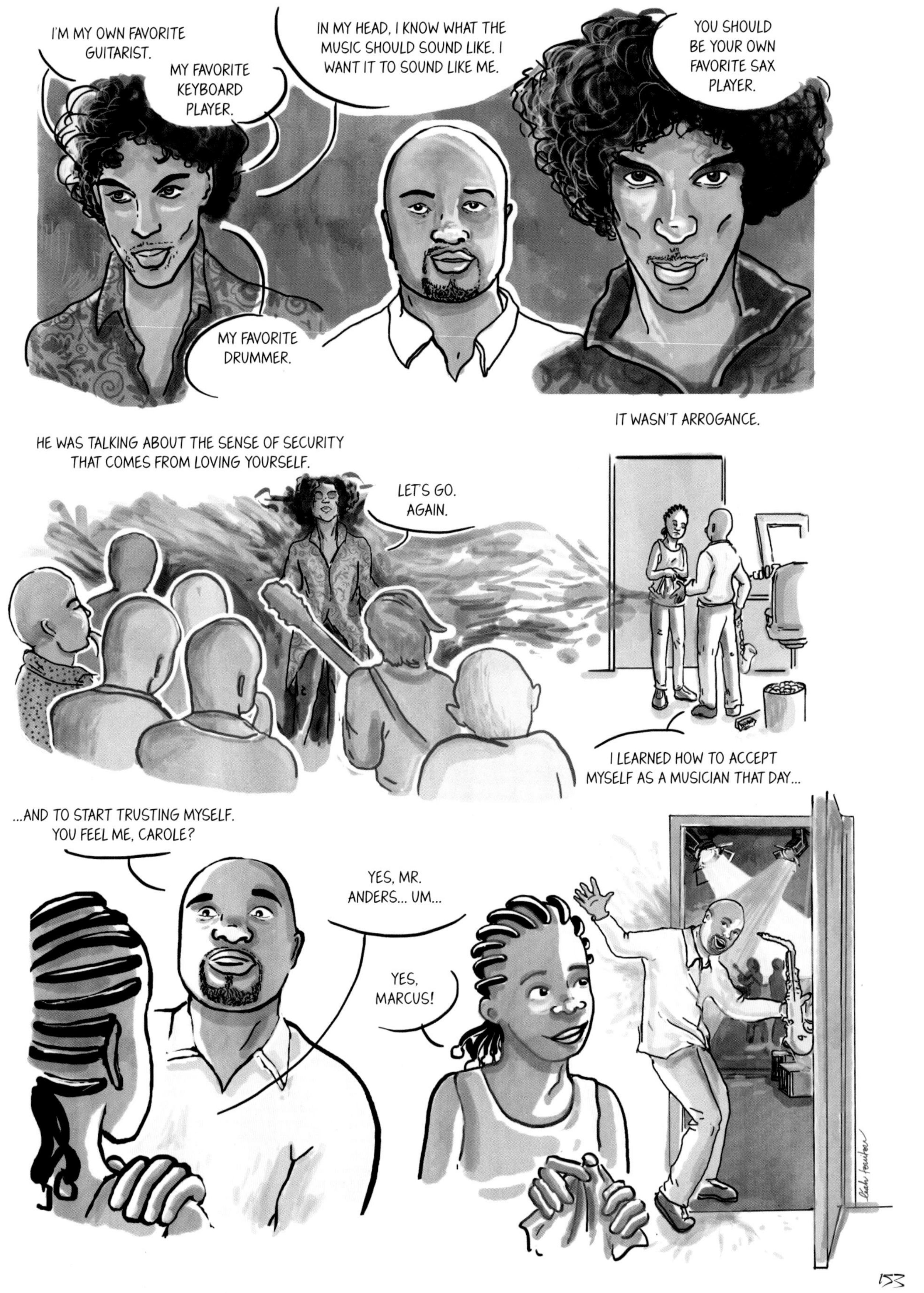
I'M MY OWN FAVORITE GUITARIST.
MY FAVORITE KEYBOARD PLAYER.
MY FAVORITE DRUMMER.
IN MY HEAD, I KNOW WHAT THE MUSIC SHOULD SOUND LIKE. I WANT IT TO SOUND LIKE ME.
YOU SHOULD BE YOUR OWN FAVORITE SAX PLAYER.
HE WAS TALKING ABOUT THE SENSE OF SECURITY THAT COMES FROM LOVING YOURSELF.
LET'S GO. AGAIN.
IT WASN'T ARROGANCE.
I LEARNED HOW TO ACCEPT MYSELF AS A MUSICIAN THAT DAY...
...AND TO START TRUSTING MYSELF. YOU FEEL ME, CAROLE?
YES, MR. ANDERS... UM...
YES, MARCUS!

This would be one of Prince's last adventures. And one of his most innovative. By the beginning of the 2010s, Prince had had it all, won it all. He had a new album out, *20Ten*, his public appearances were highly praised, the prizes and awards were piling up (*Time Magazine* ranked him among the world's one hundred most influential people) and a gigantic new tour, the Welcome 2 America Tour, attracted huge crowds every step of the way. One hundred and fifteen concerts or after-shows between December 15, 2010 and September 26, 2012, in the U.S., Canada, Europe (15 countries!) and Australia. The New Power Generation was killing it behind the boss with funk, jazz, and soul—the whole package, in other words. Prince was at the height of his popularity. So what happened? We will never know whether or not a certain level of weariness had finally caught up with him. But whatever the reason, 2013 kicked off with the announcement of a new band. A girl band, a *small* girl band (only three musicians!), and…wait for it…they played rock! The 3rdeyegirl line up: Hannah Ford on drums, Donna Grantis on guitar and Ida Nielsen on bass.

Person of the Year

PRINCE
The Genius

Recognition in the form of media validation: the prestigious *Time Magazine* named Prince Person of the Year, calling him a "genius." Who can top that?

THE BAND CHOSEN BY PRINCE TO ACCOMPANY HIM DURING THE LAST CHAPTER OF HIS LIFE CAUGHT EVERYONE OFF GUARD: AN AMATEUR BAND, AN ALL-FEMALE BAND, WHICH, TO TOP IT ALL OFF, PLAYED ROCK... AND PLAYED IT LOUD!

Hardly anyone knew anything about this amateur combo. But on the other hand, all Prince's fans were well aware of his long-standing love of rock. He had always said that rock, one of the dominant music genres available to kids his age during his teenage years in Minneapolis, undeniably played a key role in shaping his musical taste and sensibilities.

Nearly forty years later, the Kid rediscovered his passion for rock 'n' roll. Forget about the synthesizers of the Minneapolis Sound and bring out the guitars! Several test concerts were put on at the Dakota Jazz Club in Minneapolis (no more than 500 seats per night, which obviously all sold out), then he moved on to serious business and embarked on a series of shows in New York, Austin, Vancouver, Seattle, Portland, and more. In addition to 3rdeyegirl's own songs, the set list favored rarely played songs and deliberately "forgot" to play the big hits. This was the Live Out Loud Tour, which played primarily in smaller venues that rarely had a seating capacity of more than a few thousand.

The splendor and power of the princely machine in Montreux, when the artist played there in 2013. Nineteen musicians on stage!

It was in Europe, at the famous festival in Montreux, Switzerland, that one of the highlights of the tour would take place. Prince had already performed twice in this temple of jazz, in 2007 then 2009. He had opted for a frankly jazzy tone for this first appearance (a single date), then a calm and melodic one for the second one (two nights). With 2013 came the third princely appearance on the shores of Lake Geneva... and a change of gear. This time, he was booked for three shows July 13, 14 and 15, 2013. The first two featured nineteen musicians on stage, including an incredible brass section. The third switched to radical rock mode with the three girls of the 3rdeyegirl – and ended with a jam session that covered almost the entire princely repertoire; a show that still gives a chill to the fans who were there that night.

Back in Minneapolis at the end of August, Prince announced the forthcoming simultaneous release of two new albums, *Art Official Age* and *Plectrum Electrum*. The first, with R&B and electro vibes, would be a typically princely record. The second was the collective work of 3rdeyegirl and, recorded as a concert, had a totally rock sound. As the man who could never get enough, this was one of Prince's last real attempts at reinventing himself. **Unfortunately, the band, except for a few concert dates in 2015, would not survive this joint collaboration for long. Neither would Prince..**

2014
ART OFFICIAL AGE

2014
PLECTRUM ELECTRUM

2016
THE END OF
ALL SONGS

No one was expecting such a stage exit... In the spring of 2016, just back from a more intimate tour that was significantly shortened due to the Paris attacks, Prince died at home, from an overdose of opioids, the painkillers causing so much devastation in the U.S. Like Mozart two and a half centuries earlier, he left behind an impressive body of work - and his mark as a genius.

ART: Barrack Rima

Fox Theater, Atlanta.
Just when he had recently developed a more soul-jazz-funk style,
Prince decided to cut it all short and dive back into his work.

"A Piano & A Microphone" was a breathtaking piano and
voice tour. He played through his repertoire alone. Exposed.

Like a swan song.

This concert of April 14, 2014 would be his last dance.

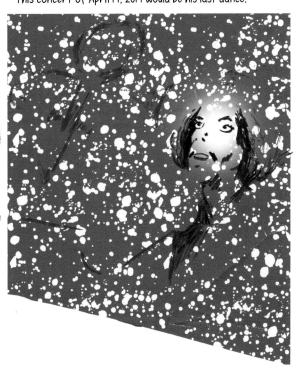

After the show on that night, Prince passed out on the flight home to Paisley Park.

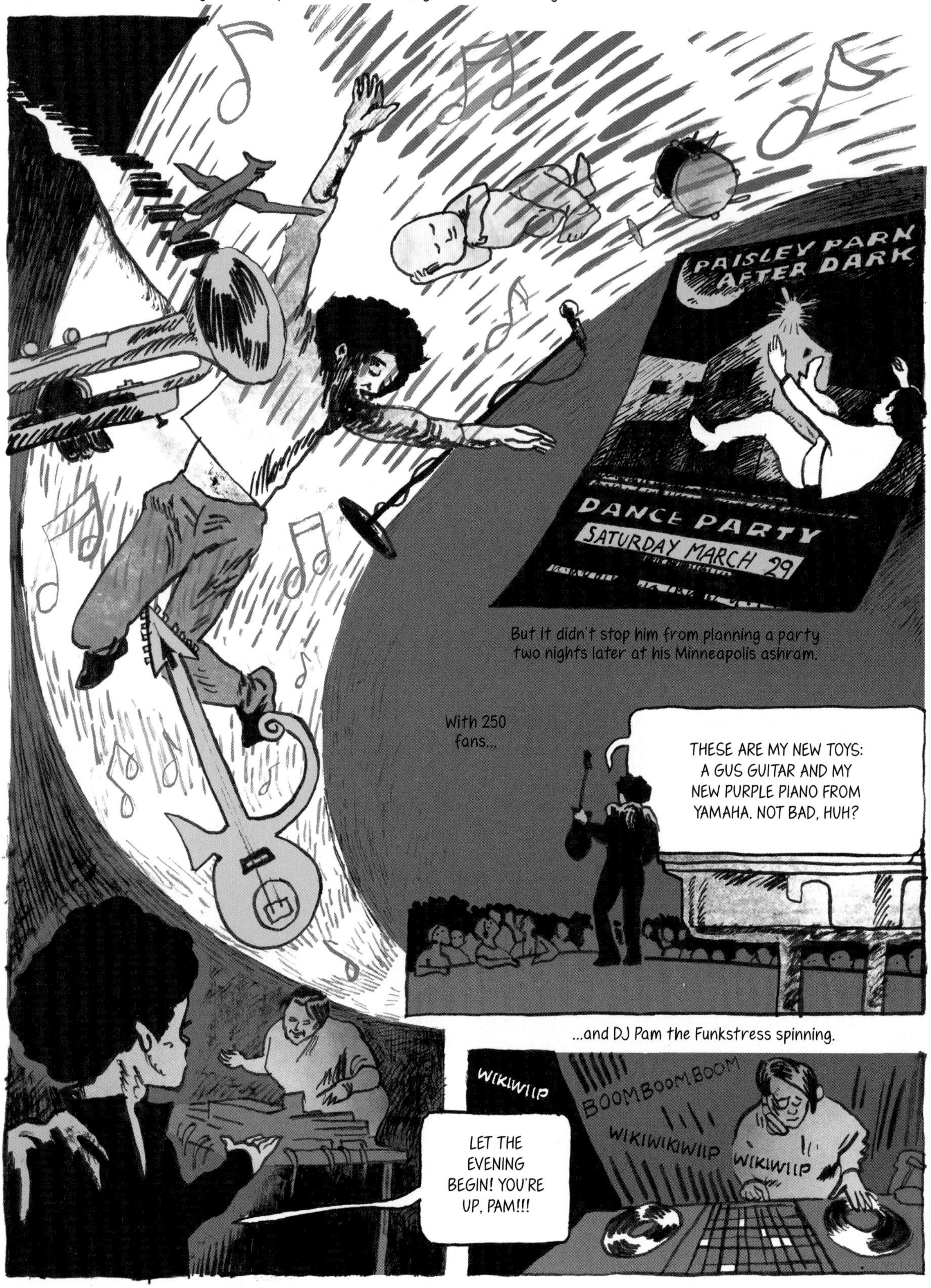
PAISLEY PARK AFTER DARK
DANCE PARTY
SATURDAY MARCH 29
But it didn't stop him from planning a party two nights later at his Minneapolis ashram.
With 250 fans...
THESE ARE MY NEW TOYS: A GUS GUITAR AND MY NEW PURPLE PIANO FROM YAMAHA. NOT BAD, HUH?
...and DJ Pam the Funkstress spinning.
WIKIWIIP
LET THE EVENING BEGIN! YOU'RE UP, PAM!!!
BOOMBOOMBOOM
WIKIWIKIWIIP
WIKIWIIP

Prince called up Dan Piepenbring on the night of the 17th.

HEY DAN, IT'S PRINCE.

HMPF... HOLD ON A SEC.

He and Dan were working on a book titled *The Beautiful Ones*.

I WANTED TO TELL YOU I'M FINE, DESPITE WHAT THE PRESS IS SAYING.

HOW WAS YOUR PARTY?

IT WAS COOL. I THANKED MY FANS FOR ALL THE GOOD TIMES, THE LOVE AND THE SUPPORT THEY GAVE ME.

As it turned out...

I TOLD THEM THEY COULD SAVE THEIR PRAYERS FOR LATER!

...Dan finished the book alone...

The Beautiful Ones.

...Because on April 21st...

...it all ended.

It was the last take for the idol.

CLAC!

Fucking painkillers...

159

Prince was an infinitely complex personality.

Generous, but with a reputation of being tough with his teams.

He simply wanted everyone to surpass themselves.

His strictness was a gift he offered his associates, which applied to his own career and to the vision he applied to his art.

To his fans, he was sometimes baffling, even incomprehensible.

But to the whole world, he offered the thrill of a work as abundant as it was masterful...

...which he probably paid for with his life.

The Vault, both a safe and a treasure trove, is something Prince fans fantasize about.

How many unreleased masterpieces does it hold? How many treasures?

Freedom, innovation, audacity...

Prince literally reinvented himself.

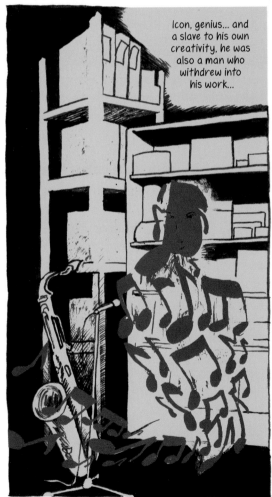

Icon, genius... and a slave to his own creativity, he was also a man who withdrew into his work...

...a man whose music we will go on listening to and whose life and career we will go on telling the way we tell legends.

Kiss.

His music will never die. It's an idea that rings out reassuringly...

...with a kind of happy ending.

Piano and a Microphone. A piano, a microphone, a voice. This was the title that Prince chose for what was to be his new tour in late 2015. We should add: and a presence, given how much the Kid from Minneapolis's aura had become, over the years and then decades, one of the essential markers of his power of attraction on stage. Scheduled to start out in Europe, this seductively titled project crashed and burned almost immediately. The attacks of September 13 in Paris cut short any hint of a European tour. Instead of what had promised to be a big party on a planetary scale, Prince and his staff downsized the tour to a much more modest scope, and confined it to the English-speaking world: only a dozen dates between January and April 2016 in the U.S., Canada and Australia/New Zealand, and then bye-bye... Because exactly one week after the final stage of the Piano & a Microphone Tour, at the Fox Theater in Atlanta, Georgia on April 14, Prince was found dead at home in one of the elevators of the Paisley Park complex. According to the local police, he had most likely suffered an overdose of Fentanyl, the powerful opioid he consumed on a regular basis.

"It is with profound sadness that I confirm that the legendary performer Prince Rogers Nelson died in his home in Paisley Park this morning," his spokesperson Yvette Noel-Schure later announced on the evening of Thursday April 21. Exit stage. Curtain.

And make way for the legend. Who exactly was this musical phenomenon capable, at the tender age of nineteen, of persuading a major music label to give him a lucrative contract even though he had no previous track record whatsoever? How can anyone understand all the parts of the sum, the equation of this secretive man of few words, who came off as borderline autistic at times yet nevertheless, in an instant, could ignite a stage and an audience while parading around in a thong, practically naked? To what do we owe all those attempts to shock and provoke, with the references to masturbation, fornication, incest that were so plentiful in his career? How to decode the Jehovah's Witness Prince? The relentless creator Prince, the virtuoso Prince?

Part of the mystery of Prince remains. Part of his dark side too, perhaps. But no one doubts that this exceptional artist has forever left his mark on all pop culture of the last half-century, building a bridge between all forms of popular musical expression. He was only five feet two, but as it says in the poem, his giant wings made it hard for him to walk..

And so Prince soared.

> HIS PRODIGIOUS 40-YEAR CAREER EVENTUALLY GOT THE BEST OF HIM: WORN-OUT BY THE PAIN-KILLERS HE ABUSED, PRINCE EXITED THE STAGE WITHOUT WARNING. ALL WE HAVE LEFT OF HIM IS HIS GARGANTUAN LEGACY.

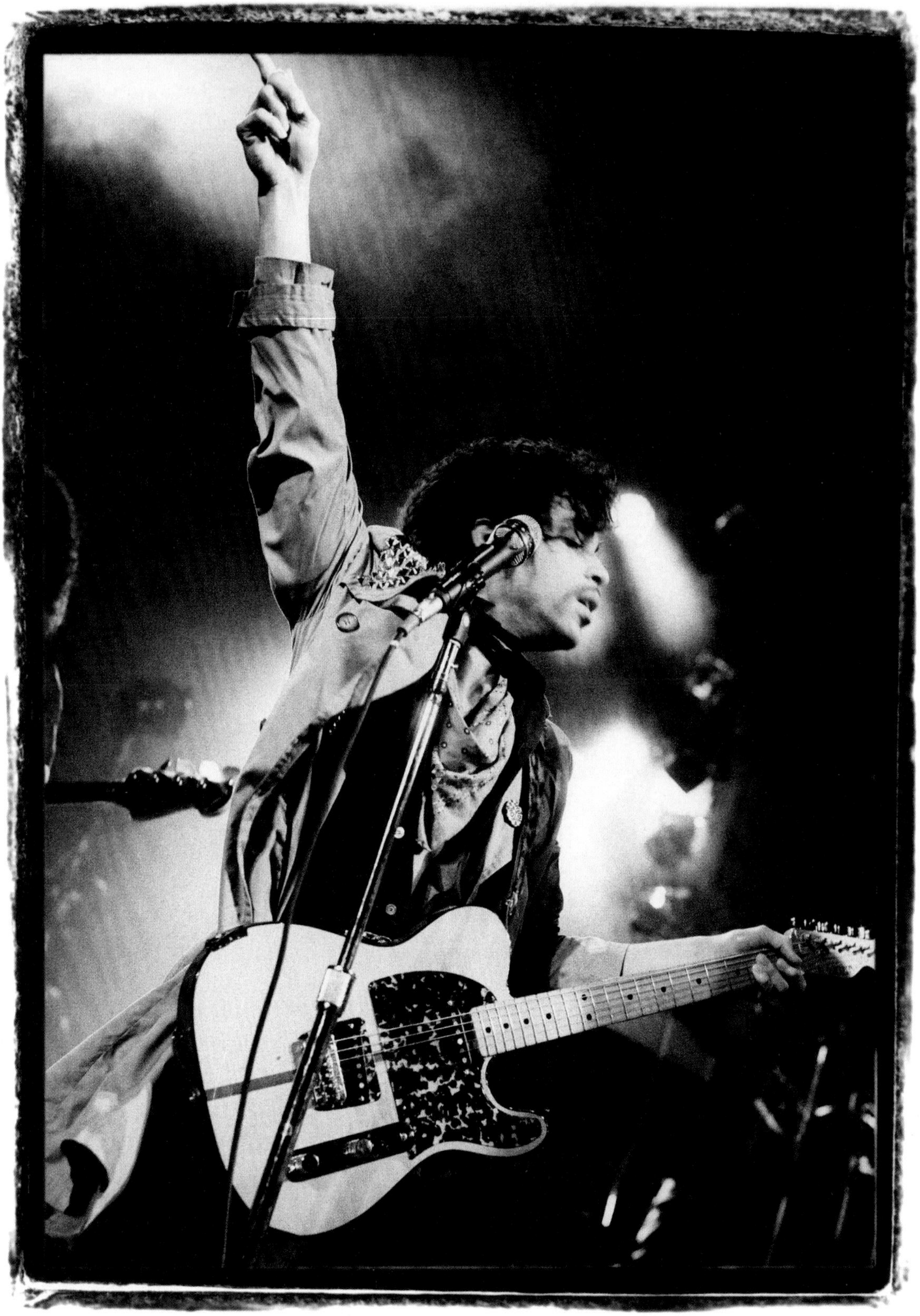

SELECT DISCOGRAPHY

Prince's discography is a lush jungle of offerings. Most sources credit him with a total of 47 albums (!) - 44 in the studio, 3 live - some of which are attributed to Madhouse or New Power Generation, without necessarily explicitly mentioning the name of the artist. They were released between 1978 for the first one (For You) and 2015 (Hitnrun Phase Two) for the last one. And that's without even taking into account the albums of other male and female artists he produced or shepherded, or the princely compositions that were performed by others than him... All of his body of work is not, however, equal quality. The crowning glory of the Minneapolis Kid's music is the 1982 - 1992 decade, almost of all of which was simply brilliant. Here is the essential Prince repertoire, as assessed by the authors of this book - in all subjectivity, of course.

Dirty Mind (1980)
Controversy (1981)
1999 (1982)
Purple Rain (1984)
Parade (1986)
Sign o'the Times (1987)
Lovesexy (1988)
Diamonds and Pearls (1991)

Love Symbol Album (1992)
The Hits/ The B Sides (1993)
Emancipation (1996)
Crystal Ball / The Truth (1998)
Rave Un2 the Joy Fantastic (1999)
The Rainbow Children (2001)
One Nite Alone... Live ! (2002)
Musicology (2004)

FILMS AND VIDEOS

In addition to the handful of feature films directed by and/or starring Prince (and which, let's face it, are rarely convincing), there is a lot of video work devoted to him (concert extracts, documentaries, etc. .), most of which can be found online. Below are the most significant films and videos.

Purple Rain (directed by Albert Magnoli, 1984)
Prince and the Revolution : Live (directed by Joseph Ruffalo, 1985, concert at the Carrier Dome in Syracuse, New York)
Under the Cherry Moon (directed by Prince, 1986)
Sign o'the Times (directed by Prince, 1987)
Lovesexy Live (directed by Egbert Van Hees, 1988)
Graffiti Bridge (directed by Prince, 1990)
Rave Un2 the Year 2000 (directed by Prince, 2000)
Live at the Aladdin Las Vegas (directed by Sanaa Hamri, 2003)
Sexy Mother F*** (directed by Oliver Schwabe, 2018)

ON THE WORLD WIDE WEB

WEBSITES
www.princevault.com
www.schkopi.com
www.calhounsquare.info
www.calhounsquare.fandom.com
WORTH CHECKING OUT ON YOUTUBE
Prince's performance at the 2007 Super Bowl Halftime show.
Prince's interview on the Oprah Winfrey Show.
Prince's guitar solo in "While My Guitar Gently Weeps" at the Rock and Roll Hall of Fame as part of a group tribute to George Harrison along with Tom Petty, Steve Winwood and others.
Prince's full interview with Tavis Smiley
Prince's interview with Arsenio Hall
SOME OF THE MOST AWESOME PRINCE MUSIC VIDEOS

Kiss
Purple Rain
1999
Little Red Corvette
I Would Die 4 You
Raspberry Beret

When Doves Cry
Let's Go Crazy
I Wanna Be Your Lover
Manic Monday (written by Prince, performed
by The Bangles)
Hot Summer

READING

Prince on Prince: Interviews and Encounters (22) (Musicians in Their Own Words) - 2022
"This book is in some ways the closest you will get to sitting down and talking with Prince. A must-have for anyone who wants to learn more about this one-of-a-kind, spectacular, creative force of nature, the likes of which we have never seen or heard before and never will again." —Jeff Munson, former Paisley Park staff and art director

My Name Is Prince - 2019 by Randee St. Nicholas
The ultimate collection of stunning photographs documenting the career of one of the world's greatest superstars.
"St. Nicholas's riveting retrospective offers a photographic tour-de-force that illustrates Prince's passion for life."
– Publishers Weekly
"St. Nicholas deftly gives a rare inside look at the infamously private Prince's personality and friendship." – Billboard

The Beautiful Ones - 2019 by Prince and Dan Piepenbring
The unfinished memoir.
"The Beautiful Ones is not a read, but an experience, an immersion inside the mind of a musical genius. You are steeped in Prince's images, his words, his essence. . . ". —USA Today (★★★★out of four stars)

The Most Beautiful: My Life With Prince - 2018 by Mayte Garcia
An intimate memoir by Prince's first wife.

I Would Die 4 U: Why Prince Became an Icon - 2019 by Touré
"A worthwhile addition to the relatively small number of decent books about Prince. It's certainly bound to be a conversation (or possibly debate) starter for serious Prince fans." —The Morton Report

INTERVIEWS AND ARTICLES

Prince Talks: The Silence Is Broken
The Purple Pleasure Palace houses the genius behind 'Around the World in a Day'
Rolling Stone

Prince's Lost Rolling Stone Interview: 'I Don't Think About Gone'
"I just think about in the future when I don't want to speak in real time," Prince says in unpublished 2014 Q&A

Prince's "Tough" Interview and the Power of Mystique
By David Kamp
Vanity Fair

How we made Prince's Purple Rain
Interviews by Michael Hann
The Guardian

ACKNOWLEDGEMENTS

Tony Lourenço would like to thank the entire Petit à Petit team, the true conductors of this book. A big thank you to Olivier Petit for his faith in me and Nicolas Finet for his insightful texts and the quality of our exchanges. A big thank you to the artists who set my scripts to music (and to Christopher for his great cover!). I would like to thank my friends Alain and Jérôme, unconditional Prince fans, for their advice. And the women in my life whom I love so much. To Prince, absolute genius... T.L.

Nicolas Finet would like to thank Romain Nélis, the artistic director of this book, who spared neither his efforts nor his talent to make each of our books the best they can be. I want to thank Olivier Petit and the Petit à Petit team for their trust in me – and a big thank also to Elisabeth Bailly, who knows why. The title of the last chapter, "The End of All Songs," was of course borrowed from Michael Moorcock. And thanks to Prince for one day composing *It Snows In April*. N.F.

**Also available from
NBM Comics Biographies:**

The Beatles in Comics
The Rolling Stones in Comics
Bob Marley in Comics
Michael Jackson in Comics
David Bowie in Comics
Queen in Comics
Mingus
Django, Hand on Fire
Love Me Please,
The Story of Janis Joplin
*"Solid art and thorough research.
Christopher's art glows when the
Summer of Love hits full bloom."*
-Publishers Weekly
Willie Nelson
*"Lovingly delivers a visual concert for
the famed musical icon, capturing
the rhythm of his life."*
-Library Journal

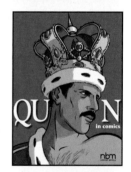

Other comics biographies from NBM:
Albert Einstein
Alfred Hitchcock
Fists Raised
Leonardo Da Vinci & The Renaissance of The World
Marie Antoinette, Phantom Queen
Niki de Saint Phalle
Philip K. Dick
Phoolan Devi
Rodin
Rosa Parks
Sartre
Tamba: Child Soldier
The Disney Bros.
The Provocative Colette
Thoreau
Women Discoverers

We have hundreds of graphic novels available.
See previews, get exclusives and order from:
NBMPUB.COM
Subscribe to our monthly newsletter
Find us on Facebook (nbmgraphicnovels),
Instagram (same), Twitter (@nbmpub).

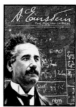
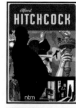

Best of recent NBM Graphic Novels:
Darkly She Goes
Hubert • Mallié
"An exciting, engaging, and emotional grand graphic novel fantasy about self-discovery, romance, and redemption."
-Foreword

Beauty
Hubert • Mallié
"Satiric, flamboyant fairy tale. Recommended for older teens and adults looking for out-of-the-way fantasy."
-Library Journal

Bluesman
Vollmar • Callejo
"[This] earthy graphic novel tells a tale worth hearing – and seeing. Bluesman, in the end, is a cathartic ghost story. Is there a better description of the blues?"
-Laurel Maury, NPR

Bootblack
Mikael
"Fans of historical thrillers and classic comics alike will delight in this tour through vintage neighborhoods so real one can almost smell the shoe polish."
-Publishers Weekly

Giant
Mikael
"Set during the construction of Rockefeller Center in the 1930s, this spectacularly drawn historical epic brings Depression-era New York City to riotous, romanticized life. Lives up to its inspiring setting, a muscular young city in a nation of immigrants, brimming with stories to tell."
-Publishers Weekly

Prince in Comics:
Lettering by Ortho
Printed in China
1st printing September 2023
**This book is also available wherever e-books are sold;
ISBN 9781681123226.**